POEMS FROM THE DIVAN OF HAFIZ

POEMS FROM THE
DIVAN OF HAFIZ

TRANSLATED BY
GERTRUDE LOWTHIAN BELL

GYAN

Published by

Gyan Publishing House
5, Ansari Road
Daryaganj, New Delhi-110002
Phone: 011-47034999, 9811692060
E-mail: books@gyanbooks.com

Distribution Network
gyanbooks.com
India, USA, Canada, UK, Australia, France

ISBN : 978-81-212-9787-5 (PB)
First Published, 1928

2nd Impression 2023

Printed at: Gyan Press, Delhi.

POMES FROM THE DIVAN OF HAFIZ
Author: GERTRUDE LOWTHIAN BELL

POEMS FROM THE
DIVAN OF HAFIZ

TRANSLATED BY

GERTRUDE LOWTHIAN BELL

WITH A PREFACE BY

E. DENISON ROSS

1928

TO

HAFIZ OF SHIRAZ

قضا دستیست پنج انگشت دارد   چه خواهد از کسي کامي برآرد
دو بر چشمش نهد دیگر دو بر گوش   یکي بر لب نهد گوید که خاموش

Thus said the Poet: " When Death comes to you,
All ye whose life-sand through the hour-glass slips,
He lays two fingers on your ears, and two
Upon your eyes he lays, one on your lips,
Whispering : Silence ! " Although deaf thine ear,
Thine eye, my Hafiz, suffer Time's eclipse,
The songs thou sangest still all men may hear.

Songs of dead laughter, songs of love once hot,
Songs of a cup once flushed rose-red with wine,
Songs of a rose whose beauty is forgot,
A nightingale that piped hushed lays divine:
And still a graver music runs beneath
The tender love notes of those songs of thine,
Oh, Seeker of the keys of Life and Death !

DEDICATION

While thou wert singing, the soft summer wind
That o'er Mosalla's garden blew, the stream
Of Ruknabad flowing where roses twined,
Carried thy voice farther than thou could'st dream.
To Isfahan and Baghdad's Tartar horde,
O'er waste and sea to Yezd and distant Ind ;
Yea, to the sun-setting they bore thy word.

Behold we laugh, we warm us at Love's fire,
We thirst and scarce dare tell what wine we crave,
We lift our voices in Grief's dark-robed choir ;
Sing thou the wisdom joy and sorrow gave !
If my poor rhymes held aught of the heart's lore,
Fresh wreaths were theirs to lay upon thy grave—
Master and Poet, all was thine before !

BIBLIOGRAPHY

SAFAR NAMEH. Persian pictures. A book of travel. Bentley, London, 1894. [Published anonymously.]

"Poems from the Divan of Hafiz." Translated by Gertrude L. Bell. Heinemann, London, 1897.

"The Desert and the Sown." By Gertrude Lowthian Bell. Heinemann, London, 1907. Two editions and a German translation.

RAMSAY (SIR W. M.) and G. L. BELL. "The Thousand and One Churches." Hodder and Stoughton, 1909.

BERCHEM (MAX VAN) AMIDA. . . (Mit einem Beitrage: "The Churches and Monasteries of the Tur Abdin" von Gertrude L. Bell.) Winter, Heidelberg, 1910.

"The Vaulting System of Ukhaidir." *Journal of Hellenic Studies*, xxx., pp. 69-81. 1910.

"Amurath to Amurath." Heinemann, London, 1911.

"Palace and Mosque at Ukhaidir." A study in Early Mohammedan Architecture. Clarendon Press, Oxford, 1914.

"Review of the Civil Administration of Mesopotamia." (India Office White Book. December, 1920.)

"Political History of Iraq," in "Encyclopædia Britannica," 13th Edition.

Also articles in *The Fortnightly Review*, *Blackwood's Magazine*, &c.

INTRODUCTION

SHEMSUDDIN MAHOMMAD, better known by his poetical surname of Hafiz, was born in Shiraz in the early part of the fourteenth century.[1] His names, being interpreted, signify the Sun of the Faith, the Praiseworthy, and One who can recite the Koran ; he is further known to his compatriots under the titles of the Tongue of the Hidden and the Interpreter of Secrets. The better part of his life was spent in Shiraz, and he died in that city towards the close of the century. The exact date either of his birth or of his death is unknown. He fell upon turbulent times. His delicate love-songs were chanted to the rude accompaniment of the clash of arms, and his dreams must have been interrupted often enough by the nip of famine in a beleaguered town, the inrush of conquerors, and the flight of the defeated.

[1] For the history of the times of Hafiz, see Defrémery in the *Journal Asiatique* for 1844 and 1845, Malcolm's "History of Persia," Price's "Mohammedan History," Markham's "History of Persia." For the life of the poet, see V. Hammer ; Defrémery in the *Journal Asiatique* for 1858 ; Sir Gore Ouseley and Daulat Shah, whose work is mainly a string of anecdote—I have been told that Lutfallah's is little better.

INTRODUCTION

The history of Persia in the fourteenth century is exceedingly confused. Beyond a succession of wars and turmoils, there is little to be learnt concerning the political conditions under which Hafiz lived. Fifty years before the birth of the poet, Hulagu, a grandson of the great Tartar invader Chinghis Khan, had conquered Baghdad, putting to death the last of the Abbaside Khalifs and extinguishing the direct line of the race that had ruled over Persia since 750. For the next 200 years there is indeed a branch of the family of Abbas living in Cairo, members of which were set up as Khalifs by the Mamluk Sultans of Egypt; but they were destitute of any real authority, and their position was that of dependants in the Mamluk court.

The sons and grandsons of Hulagu succeeded him as lords of Persia and Mesopotamia, paying a nominal allegiance to the Great Khan of the Mongols in Cambalec or Pekin, but for all practical purposes independent, and the different provinces of their empire were administered by governors in their name. About the time of the birth of Hafiz, that is to say in the beginning of the fourteenth century, a certain Mahmud Shah Inju was governing the province of Fars, of which Shiraz is the capital, in the name of Abu Said, the last of the direct descendants of Hulagu. On the death of Mahmud Shah, Abu Said appointed Sheikh Hussein ibn Juban to the governorship of Fars, a lucrative and much-coveted post. Sheikh Hussein took the precaution of ordering the three sons of Mahmud Shah to be seized and imprisoned ; but while they were passing through the streets of Shiraz in the hands of their captors, their mother, who accompanied them, lifted her veil and made a touching appeal to the people, calling upon them to remember the benefits they had received from their late ruler, the father of the three boys. Her words took instant effect ; the inhabitants rose, released her and her sons, and drove Sheikh Hussein into exile. He, however, returned with an army supplied by Abu Said, and induced Shiraz to submit again to his rule. In 1335, a year or two after these events, Abu Said died, and the power of the house of Hulagu crumbled away. There followed a long period of anarchy, which was brought to an end when Oweis, another descendant of Hulagu, seized the throne. He and his son Ahmed reigned in Baghdad until Ahmed was driven out by the invading army of Timur. But during the years of anarchy the authority of the Sultan of Baghdad had been considerably curtailed. On Abu Said's death, Abu Ishac, one of the three sons of Mahmud Shah Inju who had so narrowly escaped from the hands of Sheikh Hussein, took possession of Shiraz and Isfahan, finally ousting his old enemy, while Mahommad ibn Muzaffar, who had earned a name for valour in the service of Abu Said, made himself master of Yezd.

From this time onward the governors of the Persian provinces seem to have given a nominal allegiance now to the Sultan of Baghdad, now to the more distant Khalif. The position of Shiraz between Baghdad and Cairo must have resembled that of Venice between Rome and Constantinople, and, like Venice, she was obedient to neither lord.

Abu Ishac had not steered his bark into quiet waters. In 1340 Shiraz was besieged and taken by a rival Atabeg, and the son of Mahmud Shah was obliged to content himself with Isfahan. But in the following year he returned, captured Shiraz by a stratagem, and again established himself as ruler over all Fars. The remaining years of his reign are chiefly occupied with military expeditions against Yezd, where Mahommad ibn Muzaffar and his sons were building up a formidable power. In 1352, determined to put an end to these attacks, Mahommad marched into Fars and laid siege to Shiraz. Abu Ishac, whose life was one of perpetual dissipation, redoubled his orgies in the face of danger. Uncertain of the fidelity of the people of Shiraz, he put to death all the inhabitants of two quarters of the town, and contemplated insuring himself of a third quarter in a similar manner. But these measures did not lead to the desired results.

The chief of the threatened quarter got wind of the King's design, and delivered up the keys of his gate to Shah Shudja, son of Mahommad ibn Muzaffar, and Abu Ishac was obliged to seek refuge a second time in Isfahan. Four years later, in 1357, he was given up to Mahommad, who sent him to Shiraz and, with a fine sense of dramatic fitness, had him beheaded in an open space before the ruins of Persepolis.

The Arab traveller Ibn Batuta, who visited Shiraz between the years 1340 and 1350, has left a description of its ruler: " Abu Ishac," says he, " is one of the best Sultans that can be found " (it must be confessed that the average of Sultans was not very high in Ibn Batuta's time); " he is fair of face, imposing of presence, and his conduct is no less to be admired. His mind is generous, his character remarkable, and he is modest although his power is great and his territories extensive. His army exceeds the number of 30,000 men, Turks and Persians. The most faithful of his subjects are the inhabitants of Isfahan; but he fears the Shirazis, who are a brave people, not to be controlled by kings, and he will not trust them with arms." [1] This view of his relations with the two towns tallies with Abu Ishac's subsequent history, and points to a con-

[1] The " Travels of Ibn Batuta," edited by Defrémery and Sanguinetti.

siderable power of observation on the part of Ibn Batuta. But he relates a tale which would seem to show that Abu Ishac was not unpopular even in Shiraz : on a certain occasion he wished to build a great gate in that city, and hearing of his desire the inhabitants vied with each other in their eagerness to satisfy it ; men of all ranks turned out to do the work, putting on their best clothes and digging the foundations with spades of silver. Abu Ishac shared the passion of the age for letters, and was anxious to be accounted a rival to the King of Delhi in his generosity to men of learning ; " but," sighs Ibn Batuta, " how far is the earth removed from the Pleiades ! " The Persian historian who describes Abu Ishac's execution, quotes a quatrain which the Atabeg is supposed to have written while he was in prison :

" Lay down thine arms when Fortune is thy foe,
'Gainst Heaven's wheel, Wrestler, try not a throw
Drink steadfastly the cup whose name is Death,
Empty the dregs upon the earth, and go."

So perished the first patron of Hafiz.

From 1353 to 1393, when Timur conquered Shiraz for the second and last time, the greater part of Persia was ruled by members of the house of Muzaffar. Scarcely a year passed undisturbed by civil war, scarcely a year in which one of the sons or grandsons of Mahommad did not suffer imprisonment or worse ills at the hands of his brothers. Mahommad himself was the first to fall. Shah Shudja seized his father while he was reading the Koran aloud with a poet of his court, and caused him to be blinded. A few years later the grim life beat itself out against the prison walls of Ka'lah-i-Safid. "Without just cause," sings Hafiz, "the victor of victors suffered imprisonment; guiltless, the mightiest head was laid low. He had overcome Shiraz and Tabriz and Irak; at the last his own hour came. He who, in the eyes of the world, was the light he had kindled (*i.e.* Mahommad's son, Shah Shudja), through those eyes which had gazed victorious upon the world, thrust the hot iron." A stern and pitiless man was this Mahommad, brave in battle, wise in council, ardent in religion, but hard and cruel beyond measure, a perfidious friend and a relentless enemy. The Persian historian, Lutfallah, relates that on several occasions he had seen criminals brought before Mahommad while the Amir was engaged in reading the Koran. Laying the book aside, he would draw his sword and kill the offenders as they stood, and then return unmoved to his devotions. Shah Shudja once asked his father whether he had killed 1000 men with his own hand. "No," replied Mahommad, "but I think that the number of them that I have slain must reach 800."

After his death, Shah Shudja reigned in Shiraz, and his brother Shah Yahya in Yezd. Shah Shudja was a man of like energy with his father, but it was an energy directed into different channels; the stern religious ardour of the elder man was changed into a spirit of frenzied dissipation in the younger. Whenever he was not engaged in conducting expeditions against his brothers and nephews, he was taking part in the wildest orgies in Shiraz. He was scarcely less cruel than Mahommad. In a fit of drunkenness he ordered one of his own sons to be blinded, and though, at the instance of his vizir, he repented and sent a second messenger hot foot after the first, it was already too late to save the boy. Before Shah Shudja's death the knell of the house of Muzaffar had sounded—Tamberlain and his Tartar hordes had advanced into Northern Persia. In 1382 Shah Shudja sent a propitiatory embassy to him with gifts—jewels and silks, horses, a scarlet daïs, a royal standard, and a Chinese umbrella; and Timur in return sent the King a robe of honour and a belt studded with jewels.

Worn out before his time with riotous living, Shah Shudja did his utmost to secure the welfare of his family before he died. He sent letters both to Timur and to Sultan Ahmed of Baghdad recommending to their protection his son Zein-el-Abeddin, his brothers, and his nephews. The curtain is drawn aside for a moment from the death-bed of the King, and an anecdote, such as Oriental historians love, reveals to us the fearless and terrible face. Hearing that his brother Ahmed was preparing to dispute the succession with Zein-el-Abeddin, he sent for him in order to persuade him to withdraw his claims. But when Ahmed entered the room where Shah Shudja lay sick to death, both brothers burst into tears, and Ahmed was so much overcome by emotion that he was obliged to withdraw. Thereupon Shah Shudja sent him a letter by the hand of a faithful servant. "The world," he said, "is like unto the shadow of a cloud and a dream of the night; for the one has no resting-place, and when the dreamer awakens there remains to him but a vain memory of the other. I foresee much disturbance in Shiraz; Kerman is the home of our fathers. I have no complaint to lay at your door; but now that I am about to fare upon a long journey, if you were to become a sower of discord, not I alone would reproach you, but God also; and our enemies would rejoice. Go therefore to Kerman and renounce this unhappy city." And Ahmed went.

Shah Shudja died in the odour of sanctity. Ten holy men were with him continually, reading the Koran aloud from end to end each day. He left behind him a name renowned for courage and for liberality. He was a poet, after the fashion of kings, and from boyhood he could repeat the Koran by heart.

The son, whose future he had spent his last hours in assuring, was not to remain for long upon the throne bequeathed to him by his father. During his short reign, Zein-el-Abeddin was engaged in defending himself from the attacks of his cousin Mansur, but in 1388 he was obliged to flee before an enemy more terrible than any he had yet known. Timur, who for several years had been hovering upon the borders of Fars, overran Southern Persia and took Shiraz. Zein-el-Abeddin sought refuge with Mansur, who repaid his confidence by imprisoning and blinding him. It must have been in the year 1388 that the celebrated interview between Hafiz and Timur took place (see note to Poem V.), and not at the time of the second conquest of Shiraz in 1393. The confusion between the two dates has led several writers to doubt the truth of the story, since it is almost certain that the poet had died before 1393. Timur bestowed Shiraz upon Shah Yahya, uncle to Mansur, and some time governor of Yezd; but no sooner was the Tartar army called away by disturbances in the northern parts of the empire than Mansur overthrew his uncle and possessed himself of Shiraz. Hafiz did not live to see the end of the drama, but the end was not far off. In 1393 Timur advanced with 30,000 picked men against Mansur. The Muzaffaride, with only 3000 or 4000 men, twice charged into the heart of the Tartar force, and at one moment Timur's own life was in danger. Mansur, who was himself fighting in the thickest of the battle, sent a message back to the wings of his army, ordering them to support his desperate charge ; but they did not obey his command. He fell fighting beneath the sword of Shah Rukh Mirza, Timur's son, leaving the conqueror to "march in triumph through Persepolis." Courage was a quality in which the descendants of Mahommad ibn Muzaffar were not deficient, but among a race of soldiers Mansur seems to have been distinguished for his reckless bearing. He, too, like the other members of his family, was a patron of learning, and it is related that he used to distribute 200 tomans daily among the poor scholars of Shiraz. Both on account of their popularity and of their bravery, Timur saw that there would be no peace for him in Shiraz while one member of the house of Muzaffar remained alive ; Mansur's survivors were put to the sword.

Through all these changes of fortune, Hafiz appears to have played the prudent, if rather unromantic part of the Vicar of Bray. The slender thread of his personal history is made up for the most part of more or less mythical anecdote. He was the son, according to one tradition, of a baker of Shiraz, in which city he was probably educated. The poet Jami says that he does not know under what Sufi doctor Hafiz studied. As a young man, however, he was one of the followers of Sheikh Mahmud Attar, who would seem to have been somewhat of a free-lance among the learned men of Shiraz. Sheikh Mahmud did not give himself up completely to the contemplative life, but combined the functions of a teacher with those of a dealer in fruit and vegetables. "Oh disciple of the tavern!" sings Hafiz, "give me the precious goblet, that I may drink to the Sheikh who has no monastery." Sheikh Mahmud's attitude doubtless brought him under the condemnation of the stricter Sufis, of the disciples of a certain Sheikh Hassan Asrakpush in particular, who, as the title of their master denotes, clad themselves only in blue garments, and declared that their minds were filled with heavenly desires, just as their bodies were clothed in the colour of heaven. Hafiz falls foul of this rival school in several of his poems. "I am the servant," he says, "of all who scatter the dregs of the cup and are clothed in one colour (that is, clothed in sincerity), but not of them whose bodies are clad in blue while black is the colour of their heart." And again: "Give me not the cup until I have torn from my breast the blue robe," by which he means that he cannot receive the teachings of true wisdom until he has divested himself of the errors of the uninitiated. From Sheikh Mahmud, perhaps, he learnt a wholesome philosophy which enabled him to see through the narrow-minded asceticism of other religious teachers, whether Sufi or orthodox, and he was not unmindful of the debt he owed him. "My Grey-Beard," he sings, "who scatters the dregs of the wine, has neither gold nor power, but God has made him both munificent and merciful." And indeed if he succeeded in unchaining the spirit of his disciple from useless prejudice, it may be admitted that the Sheikh went far towards providing him with a good equipment for life. Although he never submitted to any strict monastic rule, Hafiz assumed the dervish habit of which he speaks so contemptuously. We must suppose that he took the precaution, which he himself recommends, of washing it clean in the wine that Sheikh Mahmud provided for him ; in other words, that he tempered his orthodoxy with the freer doctrines he had derived from his teacher. He also became a sheikh.

How he first revealed his inimitable gift of song is not known. There is a tradition that upon a certain day one of his uncles was engaged in composing a poem upon Sufiism, and being but a mediocre poetaster, could get no further than the first line. Hafiz took up the sheet in his uncle's absence and completed the verse. The uncle was not a little annoyed ; he bade Hafiz finish the poem, and at the same time cursed him and his works. " They shall bring insanity," he declared, " upon all that read them." Men say that the curse still hangs over the Divan, therefore let no one whose reason is not strongly seated venture to study the poet. Whatever were his beginnings, it was not long before the young man rose into high repute. Abu Ishac was his first patron. " By the favour of the victorious standards of a king," says Hafiz, " I was uplifted like a banner among the makers of verse." There is a long poem addressed to Abu Ishac, in which he is called the King under whose feet the garden of his kingdom bursts into flower. " Oh great and holy ! " cries the poet, " every man who is a servant of thine is uplifted so high that the stars of Gemini are but as his girdle." Hafiz must have been in Shiraz when Abu Ishac was brought thither, a prisoner, from Isfahan ; he may even have witnessed his execution outside Persepolis. " Fate overtook him," he sighs, " all too speedily—alas for the violence and oppression in this world of pitfalls ! alas for the grace and the mercy that dwelt among us ! Hast thou not heard, oh Hafiz, the laugh of the strutting partridge ? Little considered be the clutching talons of the falcon of death."

From the protection of Abu Ishac, Hafiz passed

into that of Shah Shudja, but the relations between the two men seem to have been somewhat strained. Shah Shudja may have distrusted the loyalty of one to whom Abu Ishac had been so good a patron; moreover, he nursed a professional jealousy of Hafiz, being himself a writer of occasional verse. The historian Khondamir tells of an interview which cannot have increased the goodwill of either interlocutor towards the other. Shah Shudja reproached Hafiz with the discursiveness of his songs. "In one and the same," he said, "you write of wine, of Sufiism, and of the object of your affections. Now this is contrary to the practice of the eloquent." "That which your Majesty has deigned to speak," replied Hafiz (laying his tongue in his cheek, though Khondamir does not mention the fact), "is the essence of the truth; yet the poems of Hafiz enjoy a wide celebrity, whereas those of some other writers have not passed beyond the gates of Shiraz." But an occasional bandying of sharp speeches, in which the King usually came off second best, did little harm to a friendship which was based upon a marked correspondence in tastes. "Since the hour," declares Hafiz, "that the wine-cup received honour from Shah Shudja, Fortune has put the goblet of joy into the hand of all wine-drinkers"; and in several poems he welcomes Shah Shudja's accession to the throne and the consequent removal of an edict against the drinking of wine: "The daughter of the grape has repented of her retirement; she went to the keeper of the peace (*i.e.* Shah Shudja) and received permission for her deeds. Forth came she from behind the curtain that she might tell her lovers that she has turned about." Partly out of gratitude, partly with an eye to future favours, Hafiz proclaimed the glory of Shah Shudja, just as he had proclaimed that of the hapless Abu Ishac, and the King was not averse from such good wishes as these from the most famous poet of the age: "May the ball of the heavens be for ever in the crook of thy polo stick, and the whole world be a playing-ground unto thee. The fame of thy goodness has conquered the four quarters of the earth; may it be for all time a guardian unto thee!"

One of Shah Shudja's vizirs, Hadji Kawameddin Hassan, was also a good friend to Hafiz. In the poems he is frequently alluded to as the second Assaf (the first Assaf having been King Solomon's vizir, renowned for his wisdom), while Shah Shudja masquerades under the title of Solomon himself. On his return from a journey, probably to Yezd, Hafiz spent some months in the house of the Vizir—induced thereto by a cogent argument. In one of the poems there is a dialogue between himself and a friend, in which the friend says to him, "When after two years' absence thy destiny has brought thee home, why comest thou not out of thy master's house ? " Hafiz replies that the road in which he walks is not of his choosing : " An officer of my judge stands, like a serpent, in ambush upon the path, and whenever I would pass beyond my master's threshold he serves me with a summons and hurries me back into my prison." He goes on to remark that under these painful circumstances he finds his master's house a sure refuge, and the servants of the Vizir useful allies against the officers of the law. " If any one proffers a demand to me there, I call to my aid the strong arm of one of the Vizir's dependants, and with a blow I cause his skull to be cleft in two." A summary manner, one would think, of dealing with the law, and little calculated to incline the heart of his judge towards the offender.

There is another Khawameddin who is frequently mentioned, the Vizir of Sultan Oweis of Baghdad. He founded in Shiraz a college for Hafiz, in which the poet gave lectures on the Koran, and read out his own verses, and whither his fame drew a great number of pupils. We find Hafiz asking his benefactor for money to support this school in the following terms : " Oh discreet friend (my poem), in some retired spot to which even the wind is a stranger, come to the ear of the master, and between jest and earnest place the pointed saying, that his heart may consent unto it ; then, of thy kindness, pray his munificence to tell me, if I were to ask for a small stipend, would my request be tolerated ?" One cannot but hope that so charming a begging letter, couched in verse withal, was more than tolerated. It was probably this Vizir who sent a robe of honour to Hafiz which, when it came, proved to be too short for him ; " but," says the poet politely, " no favour of thine could be too short for any man."

From Oweis himself Hafiz is said to have received kindness, but he does not seem to have been satisfied with the Sultan's conduct towards him : " From my heart," he says, " I am the slave of Sultan Oweis, but he remembers not his servant." The son of Oweis, Sultan Ahmed of Baghdad, whose cruelty caused his subjects to call in the aid of Timur against him, was very anxious to induce Hafiz to visit his court ; but Hafiz, perhaps with prudence, declined the invitation, saying that he was content with dry bread eaten at home, and had no desire to taste the honey that pilgrims gather by the roadside. He sent to Ahmed a poem in which he loaded his name with extravagant praise. " On Persian soil," he declared, " the bud of joy has never blown for me. How excellent is the Tigris of Baghdad and the perfumed wine ! Oh wind of the dawn, bring unto me the dust from my friend's threshold, that Hafiz may wash bright with it the eyes of his heart."

Once only did he comply with the invitations of foreign kings, and his experience on that occasion was far from encouraging. He visited Shah Yahya, Shah Shudja's brother, at Yezd, but the reward which he received was not commensurate with his expectations. " Long life to thee and thy heart's desire, oh Cup-bearer of Djem's court ! " he writes —and the context shows that the allusion is to Shah Yahya—" though while I dwelt with thee my cup was never filled with wine." Moreover, a devoted lover of Shiraz, Hafiz was overcome with home-sickness when he was absent from his native town. " Why," he says in a pathetic little poem written while he was at Yezd—" Why should I not return to mine own home ? Why should I not lay my dust in the street of mine own beloved ? My bosom cannot endure the sorrows of exile ; let me return to mine own city, let me be master of my heart's desire." It was after this luckless visit to Shah Yahya that he is said to have remarked, " It seems that Fortune did not intend kings to be wise."

He never again gathered the honey of the roads of pilgrimage. Once, indeed, in answer to the pressing invitation of Shah Mahmud Purabi, Sultan of Bengal, he set forth for India ; but a series of accidents befell him, he lost heart and returned home again. The story is told in a note to Poem XXI.

From the Sultan of Hormuz he received many favours, though he refused to visit him and his pearl fisheries in the Persian Gulf. He compares this Sultan with Shah Yahya, much to the disadvantage of the latter, saying that the King who had never seen him had filled his mouth with pearls, whereas Shah Yahya, to whose court he had journeyed, had sent him empty away.

Shah Shudja was not the only member of the house of Muzaffar who protected Hafiz ; the warrior prince Mansur was his staunch friend. He appears to have been absent from Shiraz at the time of Mansur's accession—perhaps he had accompanied Timur's retreating army. " The wind has brought me word," he cries, " that the day of sorrow is overpast ; I will return to Shiraz through the favour of my friend. On the banners of the Conqueror (*i.e.* Mansur, of whose name this is the meaning) Hafiz is borne up into heaven ; fleeing for refuge, his destiny has set him upon the steps of a throne." Mansur held the poet in high esteem. There is a tradition that when he appointed one of his sons governor over a province, the young man asked his father to give him his vizir, Jelaleddin, as a counsellor, and Hafiz as a teacher. " What ! " replied Mansur, " wouldst thou be King even in thy father's lifetime, that thou demandest of him the two wisest men in his realm ? "

Hafiz by this time had grown old. Youth had been very pleasant ; not without a sigh the grey-haired man relinquished it. " Ah, why has my black hair turned white ! " he laments, and tries to warm his old blood with the wine of former days. " Yesterday at dawn I came upon one or two glasses of wine—as sweet as the lip of the Cup-bearer they seemed to my palate. And then, my brain afire, I desired to return to my mistress, Youth, but between us a divorce had been pronounced." And again : " Last night Hafiz strayed into the tavern, and it seemed to him that Youth, his mistress, had come back, and that love and madness had returned to his old head." " Gieb meine Jugend mir zurück ! " Other poets besides Hafiz have sung to the same tune. Whether or no he lived to witness the overthrow of the race that had sheltered him, he foresaw the troubles that were coming upon it and upon his beloved Shiraz. There is a short poem full of foreboding which is said to have been written after the entry of Timur : " What tumult I see beneath the moon's orbit, every quarter of the earth is full of evil and wickedness ! There is strife among our daughters, and among our mothers contention, and the father is evilly disposed towards his son. Only the foolish are drinking sherbet of rose-water and sugar ; the wise are nourished upon their own heart's blood. The Arabian horse is wounded beneath the saddle, and the ass wears a collar of gold about his neck. Master, take the counsel of Hafiz: 'Go and do good!' for I see that this maxim is worth more than a treasure-house of jewels." In several verses he congratulates Mansur upon a victory and a fortunate return to Shiraz, which may perhaps refer to the re-establishment of the Muzaffaride line after Timur's departure. "Give me the cup," he says in one of these, "for the airs of youth blow through my old head, so glad am I to see the King's face again."

The date of his death is variously given as 1388, 1389, 1391, and 1394, but it seems unlikely that he should have been alive as late as 1394. 1389 is the year given in a couplet by an unknown author, which is inscribed upon his tomb: "If thou wouldst know when he sought a home in the dust of Mosalla, seek his date in the dust of Mosalla." The letters of the Persian words Khak-i-Mosalla, dust of Mosalla, give the number 791, that is 1389 of our era. He lies in the garden of Mosalla outside Shiraz, a garden the praises of which he was never tired of singing, and on the banks of the Ruknabad, where he had so often rested under the shade of cypress-trees. When, some sixty years after the poet's death, Sultan Baber conquered Shiraz, he erected a monument over the tomb of Hafiz. An oblong block of stone on which are carved two songs from the Divan, marks the grave. At the head of it is inscribed a sentence in Arabic: "God is the enduring, and all else passes away." The garden contains the tombs of many devout Persians who have desired to rest in the sacred earth which holds the bones of the poet, and his prophecy that his grave should become a place of pilgrimage for all the drunkards of the world has been to a great extent fulfilled. A very ancient cypress, said to be of Hafiz's own planting, stood for many hundreds of years at the head of his grave, and "cast its shadow o'er the dust of his desire."

It is not often that a teacher and the favourite of princes enjoys unmixed popularity, especially when his criticisms of such as disagree with him are as harsh and as often repeated as are those of Hafiz; nor does he seem to have been an exception to the general rule. Moreover, his own conduct gave his enemies sufficient grounds for complaint. His biographers, as biographers will, take a rosy view of his life. Daulat Shah, for instance, states that "he turned always to the company of dervishes and of wise men, and sometimes he attained also to the society of princes; a friend of persons of eminent virtue and perfection, and of noble youths." But such accounts as these are not entirely borne out by other traditions, and his poems do not seem to the unbiased reader to be the works of a man of ascetic temperament. With all due deference to Daulat Shah, I would submit that Abu Ishac, Shah Shudja, and Shah Mansur were none of them persons of eminent virtue ; indeed, it is difficult to imagine that a friend and panegyrist of theirs could have renounced all the joys of life. His enemies went so far as to accuse him of heresy and even of atheism, and so strong was popular feeling against him that, on his death, it was debated whether his body might be given the rites of burial. The question was only settled by consulting his poems, which, on being taken at haphazard, opened upon the following verse : " Fear not to follow with pious feet the corpse of Hafiz, for though he was drowned in the ocean of sin, he may find a place in paradise." It is a fortunate age which will allow a man's writings to stand his doubtful reputation in such good stead.

Hafiz was married and he had a son. He laments the death of both wife and child in two poems which are translated in this volume. In spite of all the favours which he received from the great men of his day, he is said to have died poor.

During his lifetime he was too busy " teaching and composing philosophical treatises," says his great Turkish editor, Sudi, " to gather together his songs ; he used to recite them in his school, expressing a wish that these pearls might be strung together for the adornment of his contemporaries." This was done after his death by his pupil Sayyed Kasim el Anwar, and the Divan of Hafiz is one of the most popular books in the Persian language. From India to Constantinople his songs are sung and repeated by all who speak the Persian tongue, and the number of his European translators shows that his uncle's curse has a special and peculiar influence in Western countries. Like the Æneid, the Divan of Hafiz is consulted as a guide to future action. There are several stories of famous men who have had recourse to these *Sortes Hafizianæ*. It is related that Nadir Shah took counsel from Hafiz's book when he was meditating an expedition against Tauris, and opened it at the following verse: "Irak and Fars thou hast conquered with thy songs, oh Hafiz; now it is the turn of Baghdad and the appointed hour of Tabriz." Nadir Shah took this as an encouragement to fresh conquest, and went on his way rejoicing.

It is not only as a maker of exquisite verse but also as a philosopher that Hafiz has gained so wide an esteem in the East. No European who reads his Divan but will be taken captive by the delicious music of his songs, the delicate rhythms, the beat of the refrain, and the charming imagery. Some of them are instinct with the very spirit of youth and love and joy, some have a nobler humanity and cry out across the ages with a voice pitifully like our own; and yet few of us will turn to Hafiz for wisdom and comfort, or choose him as a guide. It is the interminable, the hopeless mysticism, the playing with words that say one thing and mean something totally different, the vagueness of a philosophy that dares not speak out, which repels the European just as much as it attracts the Oriental mind. "Give us a working theory," we demand. "Build us imaginary mansions where our souls, fugitives from the actual, may dream themselves away"—that, it seems to me, is what the Persian asks of his teacher.

Hafiz belonged to the great sect from which so many of the most famous among Persian writers have sprung. Like Sa'di and Jami and Jelaleddin Rumi and a score of others, he was a Sufi. The history of Sufiism has yet to be written, the sources from which it arose are uncertain, and that it should have found a home in Mahommadanism, the least mystical of all religions, is still unexplained. Some have supposed that Sufiism was imported from India after the time of Mahommad; some that it was a development of the doctrines of Zoroaster which the Prophet's successors silenced but did not destroy. In reply to the first theory it has been objected that there is no historic proof of relations between India and Mahommadan countries after the Mahommadan era and before the rise of Sufiism, by which the doctrines of the Indian mystics could have been propagated ; and as for the second, it seems improbable that Sufiism, of which the essential doctrine is unity, could have borrowed much from a religion as sharply opposed to it as that of Zoroaster, whose creed is founded upon a dualism. A third theory is that the origins of Sufiism are to be looked for in the philosophy of the Greeks, strangely distorted by the Eastern mind, and in the influence of Christianity ; but though the works of Plato are frequently quoted by mystical writers, and though it seems certain that they owe something both to the Neo-Platonic school of Alexandria and to the Christian religion, this would not be enough to account for the great perversion of Mahommad's teaching.

Baron Sylvestre de Sacy suggested the following explanation of the matter.[1] The second century of the Hejira was a time of fermentation and of the rise of sects. This was due in the first place to the introduction of Greek philosophy, and in the second to the rivalry between the partisans of Ali and those of the Ommiad and Abbaside Khalifs. It was among the followers of Ali that the doctrines of the union of God and man, the infusion of the Divinity in the imams, and the allegorical interpretation of religious ceremonies grew up. Daulat Shah in his Biography of the Persian Poets traces back mysticism

[1] *Journal des Savants* for 1821 and 1822.

as far as to Ali himself, though it is probable that he is imputing to the son-in-law of the Prophet beliefs which were of a somewhat later date. By force of circumstances the Alides were placed in opposition to the ruling Khalifs, and were obliged to find a justification for their attitude, and for submitting to the observances enjoined by those whom they refused to recognise as true representatives of Mahommad. They read the Koran by the light of a new creed, and interpreted it in a manner far different from that intended by its author. From the moment when the division between Shi'ite and Sunni sprang into being, the Shi'ites, or followers of Ali, made the eastern provinces of the Khalifate their stronghold. It is not unreasonable to suppose that a mysticism, in every way contrary to the true spirit of the Koran, made in those provinces nearest to India so rapid a progress, because, before the conquest of Persia by the Arabs, Indian mysticism had already struck root there. That is to say, that there had grown up, side by side with Zoroastrianism, a mysticism eminently congenial to the peculiar temper of the Persian mind—so congenial, indeed, that it was not stamped out by the Arab conquerors, but insinuated itself into the stern and practical creed which they forced upon a nation of dreamers and metaphysicians. The author of the Dabistan, a book written in the seventeenth century, containing the description of twelve different faiths, relates that there existed in Persia a sect belonging to the Yekaneh Bina, of those whose eyes are fixed upon One alone : " They say that the world has no external or tangible existence ; all that is, is God, and beyond him there is nothing. The intelligences and the souls of men, the angels, the heavens, the stars, the elements, and the three kingdoms of nature exist only in the mind of God and have no existence beyond." " If this Indian doctrine of Maya, or Illusion," adds M. de Sacy, " had been transferred to Persia, there is every reason to believe that mysticism, grounded on the doctrine that all things are an emanation from God and that unto him they shall return, may be traced to the same source."

The keynote of Sufiism is the union, the identification of God and man. It is a doctrine which lies at the root of all spiritual religions, but pushed too far it leads to pantheism, quietism, and eventually to nihilism. The highest good to which the Sufis can attain, is the annihilation of the actual—to forget that they have a separate existence, and to lose themselves in the Divinity as a drop of water is lost in the ocean.[1] In order to obtain this end

[1] Numberless beautiful images are used to describe the union of God and man. Jelaleddin Rumi points the same moral in the following exquisite apologue : " There came one and knocked at the door of the Beloved. And a voice answered and said, ' Who is there ? ' The lover replied, ' It is I.' ' Go

they recommend ascetic living and solitude ; but they do not carry asceticism to the absurd extremes enjoined by the Indian mystics, nor do they approve of artificial aids for the subduing of consciousness, such as opium, or hashish, or the wild physical exertions of the dancing dervishes. The drunkenness of the Sufi poets, say their interpreters, is nothing but an ecstatic frame of mind, in which the spirit is intoxicated with the contemplation of God just as the body is intoxicated with wine. According to the Dabistan there are four stages in the manifestation of the Divinity : in the first the mystic sees God in the form of a corporal being ; in the second he sees him in the form of one of his attributes of action, as the Maker or the Preserver of the world ; in the third he appears in the form of an attribute which exists in his very essence, as knowledge or life ; in the fourth the mystic is no longer conscious of his own existence. To the last he can hope to attain but seldom.

This losing of the soul in God is only a return (and here we come near to such Platonic doctrines as those embodied in the Phædrus) to the conditions which existed before birth into the world. Just as in the Dialogue the immortal steed which is har-

hence,' returned the voice ; 'there is no room within for thee and me.' Then came the lover a second time and knocked, and again the voice demanded, 'Who is there ?' He answered, It is thou.' 'Enter,' said the voice, 'for I am within.'"

nessed to the chariot of the soul, longs to return to the plain of birth, and to see again the true justice, beauty, and wisdom of which it has retained an imperfect recollection, so the soul of the Sufi longs to return to God, from whom it has been separated by the mortal veil of the body. But this reunion is pushed much further by the Eastern philosophers than by Plato ; it implies, according to them, the complete annihilation of distinct personality, corresponding to the conditions, quite unlike those described by the Platonic Socrates, which they believe to have existed before birth. There is nothing which is not from God and a part of God. In himself he contains both being and not being ; when he chooses he casts his reflection upon the void, and that reflection is the universe. There is a fine passage in Jami's Yusuf and Zuleikha in which he sets forth this doctrine of the creation. " Thou art but the glass," the poet concludes, " his is the face reflected in the mirror ; nay, if thou lookest steadfastly, thou shalt see that he is the mirror also." In a parable, Jami illustrates the universal presence of God, and the blind searching of man for that by which he is surrounded on every side. There was a frog which sat upon the shores of the ocean, and ceaselessly day and night he sang its praise. " As far as mine eyes can see," he said, " I behold nothing but thy boundless surface." Some fish swimming in the shallow water heard the frog's song, and were filled with a desire to find that wonderful ocean of which he spoke, but go where they would they could not discover it. At last, in the course of their search, they fell into a fisherman's net, and as soon as they were drawn out of the water they saw beneath them the ocean for which they had been seeking. With a leap they returned into it.

The story of the creation as told in the Koran it is impossible for the Sufis to accept ; they are bound to give an outward adhesion to it, but in their hearts they treat it as an allegory. The world is posterior to God only in the nature of its existence and not in time : the Sufis were not far from the doctrine of the eternity of matter, from which they were only withheld by the necessity of conforming with the teaching of the Koran. They content themselves with saying that the world came into existence when it pleased God to manifest himself beyond himself, and will cease when it shall please him to return into himself again. It is more difficult to dispose of the resurrection of the body, which is constantly insisted upon by Mahommad. That the soul, when it has at last attained to complete union with God, should be obliged to return to the prison from whence it has escaped at death, is entirely repugnant to all Sufis ;

nor can they explain satisfactorily the divergence of their opinions from those of the Prophet.

It has been well said that all religious teachers who have honestly tried to construct a working formula, have found that one of their greatest difficulties lay in reconciling the all-powerfulness of God with man's consciousness of his will being free ; for on the one hand it is impossible to conceive a God worth the name who shall be less than omnipotent and omniscient, and on the other it is essential to lay upon man some responsibility for his actions.[1] Mahommad more especially, as Count Gobineau points out in his excellent little book,[2] found himself confronted with this difficulty, since his primary object was to exalt the divine personality, and to lift it out of the pantheism into which it had fallen among the pre-Islamitic Arabs ; but if he did not succeed in indicating a satisfactory way out of the dilemma, it is at least unjust to accuse him of having failed to recognise it. He insisted that man is responsible for his own salvation : " Whosoever chooseth the life to come, their desire shall be acceptable unto God." [3] There is a tradition that

[1] Dr. Johnson's contribution to this vexed question is perhaps as good as any other : " Sir," said he to Boswell, " we *know* the will is free, there's an end on't."

[2] *Les Religions de l'Asie Centrale.*

[3] *Cf.* St. Paul, who is scarcely more explicit : " Work out your own salvation ; for it is God which worketh in you both to will and to work for his good pleasure " (Phil. ii. 12).

when some of his disciples were disputing over predestination, he said to them: "Why do you not imitate Omar? For when one came to him and asked him, 'What is predestination?' he answered, 'It is a deep sea.' And a second time he replied, 'It is a dark road.' And a third time, 'It is a secret which I will not declare since God has seen fit to conceal it.'" The Sufis were obliged to abandon free will: it was impossible to attach any responsibility to the reflection in the mirror. But here, again, they did not venture to give expression to their real opinions, and their statements are therefore both confused and contradictory. "A man may say," remarks the author of the Dabistan, "that his actions are his own, and with equal truth that they are God's." In the Gulshen-i-Raz, a poem written in the year 1317, and therefore contemporary with Hafiz, it is distinctly laid down that God will take men's actions into account: "After that moment (*i.e.* the Day of Judgment) he will question them concerning good and evil." But such expressions as these are in direct opposition to the rest of Sufi teaching. There is neither good nor evil, since both alike flow from God, from whom all flows. Some go so far as to prefer Pharaoh to Moses, Nimrod to Abraham, because they say that though Pharaoh and Nimrod were in apparent revolt against the Divinity, in reality they knew their own nothingness and accepted the part that the divine wisdom had imposed upon them. There is neither reward nor punishment; Paradise is the beauty, Hell the glory of God, and when it is said that those in Hell are wretched, it is meant that the dwellers in Heaven would be wretched in their place.[1] And finally, there is no distinction between God and man; the soul is but an emanation from God, and a man is therefore justified in saying with the fanatic Hallaj, "I am God." Though Hallaj paid with his life for venturing to give voice to his opinion, he was only repeating aloud what all Sufis believe to be true.[2] "Is is permitted to a tree to say, 'I am God,'" writes the author of the Gulshen-i-Raz (the allusion is to the burning bush that spoke to Moses); "why then may not a man say it?" And again: "In God there is no distinction of quality; in his divine majesty I, thou, and we shall not be found. I, thou, we, and he bear the same meaning, for in unity there is no division. Every man who has annihilated the body and is entirely

[1] Dabistan.

[2] Hallaj lived in the ninth century. He was believed by some to be a sorcerer, and by others a holy worker of miracles. He was condemned to death with horrible tortures by the Khalif of Baghdad in 919, and his ashes were thrown into the Tigris. It is said that a Sufi once asked God why he suffered his servant Hallaj to fall into the Khalif's hands, and was answered, "Thus the revealers of secrets are punished."

separated from himself, hears within his heart a voice that crieth, ' I am God.' "

The conception of the union and interdependence of all things divine and human is far older than Sufi thought. It goes back to the earliest Indian teaching, and Professor Deussen, in his book on Metaphysics, has pointed out the conclusion which is drawn from it in the Veda. " The gospels," he says, " fix quite correctly as the highest law of morality, Love thy neighbour as thyself. But why should I do so, since by the order of nature I feel pain and pleasure only in myself, not in my neighbour ? The answer is not in the Bible (this venerable book being not yet quite free from Semitic realism), but it is in the Veda : You shall love your neighbour as yourselves because you *are* your neighbour ; a mere illusion makes you believe that your neighbour is something different from yourselves. Or in the words of the Bhagaradgitah : He who knows himself in everything and everything in himself, will not injure himself by himself. This is the sum and tenor of all morality, and this is the standpoint of a man knowing himself a Brahman."

The Sufis were forced to pay an exaggerated deference to the Prophet and to Ali in order to keep on good terms with the orthodox, but since they believed God to be the source of all creeds they could not reasonably place one above another ; nay more, since they taught that any man who practised a particular religion had failed to free himself from duality and to reach perfect union with God, they must have held Mahommadanism in like contempt with all other faiths. " When thou and I remain not (when man is completely united with God), what matters the Ka'ba and the Synagogue and the Monastery ? "[1] That is, what difference is there between the religion of Mahommadan, Jew, and Christian ? " One night," says Ferideddin Attar in a beautiful allegory, " the angel Gabriel was seated on the branches of a tree in the Garden of Paradise, and he heard God pronounce a word of assent. ' At this moment,' thought the angel, ' some man is invoking God. I know not who he is ; but this I know, that he must be a notable servant of the Lord, one whose soul is dead to evil and whose spirit lives.' Then Gabriel desired to know who this man could be, but in the seven zones he found him not. He traversed the land and the sea and found him not in mountain or in plain. Therefore he hastened back to the presence of God, and again he heard him give a favourable answer to the same prayers. Again he set forth and sought through the world, yet he saw not the servant of God. ' Oh Lord,' he cried, ' show me the path that leads to him upon

[1] Gulshen-i-Raz.

whom thy favours fall!' 'Go to the Land of Rome,' God answered, 'and in a certain monastery thou shalt find him.' Thither fled Gabriel, and found him whom he sought, and lo! he was worshipping an idol. When he returned, Gabriel opened his lips and said, 'Oh Master, draw aside for me the veil from this secret: why fulfillest thou the prayers of one who invokes an idol in a monastery?' And God replied, 'His spirit is darkened and he knows not that he has missed the way; but since he errs from ignorance, I pardon his fault: my mercy is extended to him, and I allow him to enter into the highest place.'"

In the language of religious mysticism, God is not only the Creator and Ruler of the world, he is also the Essentially Beautiful and the True Beloved. Love, of which the divine being is at once the source and the object, plays a large part in Sufi writings, a part which it is difficult, and sometimes unwise, to distinguish from an exaggerated expression of the human affections. Jami describes Pure Being, before it had been manifested in Creation, "singing of love unto itself in a wordless melody," [1] and in the same strain Hafiz sings of "the Imperial Beauty which is for ever playing the game of love with itself." Like the echo of a Greek voice falls Jami's doctrine of human love: "Avert not thy face from

[1] Yusuf and Zuleikha.

an earthly beloved, since even this may serve to raise thee to the love of the True." It is almost possible to read in the Persian poem the words of the wise Diotima to Socrates: "He who has been instructed thus far in the things of love, and has learnt to see the Beautiful in true order and succession, when he comes towards the end will suddenly perceive a nature of wonderful beauty, not growing or decaying, waxing or waning . . . he who, under the influence of true love, rising upward from these things begins to see that beauty, is not far from the end."

The Sufis had no difficulty in finding in the Koran texts in support of their teaching. When Mahommad exclaims, "There are times when neither cherubim nor prophet are equal unto me!" the Sufis declare that he alludes to moments of ecstatic union with God; and his account of the victory of Bedr—"Thou didst not slay them, but God slew them, and thou didst not shoot when thou didst shoot, but God shot"—they take as a proof of the Prophet's belief in the essential oneness of God and man.[1] The whole book is twisted after this fashion into agreement with their views.

Beautiful and spiritual as some of these doctrines are, they can hardly be said to form an adequate guide to conduct. The Sufis, however, are regarded

[1] "A Year among the Persians." Browne.

in the East as men leading a virtuous and pure life. Even the etymology of their name points to the same conclusion : Sufi comes from an Arabic word signifying wool, and indicates that they were accustomed to clothe themselves in simple woollen garments. They occupy in the East much the same position that Madame Guyon and the Jansenists occupied in the West, and they teach the same doctrine of quietism, which, while it lends to its followers the virtues of exaggerated submission, saps the root of a faith that is manifested in works. So far as the Sufis are striving earnestly after union with God, they are saved from the logical consequences of their doctrines : " Their ear is strained to catch the sounds of the lute, their eyes are fixed upon the cup, their bosoms are filled with the desire of this world and of the world to come."[1] And in the same spirit Hafiz sings : " Though the wind of discord shake the two worlds, mine eyes are fixed upon the road from whence cometh my Friend." The idealism of the Sufis led them to deny the morality of all actions, but they restricted the consequences of their principles to the adepts who had attained to perfect union with God, and even for them the moments of ecstasy are few. Most Sufis are good and religious men, holding it their duty to conform outwardly, and no discredit to use

[1] Sayyed Ahmed of Isfahan.

all artifices to conceal from the orthodox the beliefs which they cherish in their heart, but holding also that the practice of the Mahommadan religion, to the rites of which they have attached symbolic meanings, is the only way to the perfection to which they aspire. Nevertheless, Count Gobineau is of opinion that quietism is the great curse of the East. "The dominant characteristic of Sufiism," he says, "is to unite by a weak chain of doctrine, ideas the significance of which is very different, so different that there is in reality but one connecting link between them, and that link is a quietism adapted to them all, a passive disposition of spirit which surrounds with a nimbus of inert sentiment all conceptions of God, of man, and of the universe. It is this quietism, and not Islam, which is the running sore of all Oriental countries."

Unfortunately, as he points out, the conditions of Oriental life are such as to enforce rather than to control a disposition to mysticism. The poets found ready to their hand a mass of vague and beautiful thought eminently suited to imaginative treatment; whether they believed in it or not they used it, and thereby popularised it, delighting, as only an Oriental can, in the necessity of veiling it with exquisite symbolism, and throwing round it a cloud of charming phrases. These phrases caught and held the Oriental ear; and the Oriental mind is faithful to a formula once accepted. Moreover, when a man looked about him and saw the vicissitudes of mortal existence—nowhere more marked than in the East—how conqueror succeeded conqueror and empire empire, how the humble was exalted and the mighty thrown from his seat, how swift was the vengeance of God in sweeping pestilence and resistless famine, and how unsparing the forces of nature, he turned to a philosophy which taught that all earthly things were alike vain—virtue and patriotism and the love of wife and child, power and beauty and the bold part played in a hopeless fight ; he remembered what he had learnt from poets and story-tellers—" Behold the world is as the shadow of a cloud and a dream of the night."

How far the Divan of Hafiz can be said to embody these doctrines, each reader must decide for himself, and each will probably arrive at a different conclusion. Between the judgment of Jami, that Hafiz was undoubtedly an eminent Sufi, and that of Von Hammer, who, playing upon his names, declared that the Sun of the Faith gave but an uncertain light, and the Interpreter of Secrets interpreted only the language of pleasure—between these two there is a wide field for differences of opinion. For my part, I cannot agree entirely either with Jami or with Von Hammer. Partly, perhaps, owing to the wise guidance of Sheikh Mahmud

Attar, partly to a natural freedom of spirit, Hafiz seems to me to rise above the narrow views of his co-religionists, and to look upon the world from a wider standpoint. The asceticism of Sufi and orthodox he alike condemns : " The ascetic is the serpent of the age ! " he cries. I think it was not only to curry favour with a king that he welcomed the accession of Shah Shudja, nor was it only to disarm the criticism of stricter Mohammadans that he described himself as a weary seeker after wisdom, praying God to show him some guiding light by which he might direct his steps. Of the two conclusions that are commonly drawn from the statement that to-morrow we die, Hafiz accepted neither unmodified by the other. " Eat and drink," seemed to him a poor solution of the mysterious purpose of human life, and an unsatisfactory sign-post to happiness ; " the abode of pleasure," he says, " was never reached except through pain." On the other hand, he was equally unwilling to despise the good things of this world. " The Garden of Paradise may be pleasant, but forget not the shade of the willow-tree and the fair margin of the fruitful field." " Now, now while the rose is with us, sing her praise ; now, while we are here to listen, Minstrel, strike the lute ! for the burden of all thy songs has been that the present is all too short, and already the unknown future is upon us." He, too, would have us cut down far reaching hope to the limit of our little day, though he cherished in his heart a more or less elusive conviction that he should find the fire of love burning still, and with a purer flame, behind the veil which his eyes could not pierce.

Be that as it may, one who sings the cool rush of the wind of dawn, the scarlet cup of the tulip uplifted in solitary places, the fleeting shadows of the clouds, and the praise of gardens and fountains and fruitful fields, was not likely to forget that even if the world is no more than an intangible reflection of its Creator, the reflection of eternal beauty is in itself worthy to be admired. I wish I could believe that such innocent delights as these, and a wholehearted desire for truth, had been enough for our poet, but I have a shrewd suspicion that the Cupbearer brought him a wine other than that of divine knowledge, and that his mistress is considerably more than an allegorical figure. How ever willing we may be to submit to the wise men of the East when they tell us that the revelry of the poems is always a spiritual exaltation, it must be admitted that the words of the poet carry a different conviction to Western ears. There is undoubtedly a note of sincerity in his praise of love and wine and boon-companionship, and I am inclined to think that Hafiz was one of those who, like Omar Khayyam, were wont to throw the garment of repentance annually into the fire of Spring. It must be remembered that the morality of his day was not that of our own, and that the manners of the East resemble but vaguely those of the West ; and though as a religious teacher Hafiz would have been better advised if he had less frequently loosened the rein of his desires, I doubt whether his songs would have rung for us with the same passionate force. After all, the poems of St. Francis of Assisi are not much read nowadays. Nevertheless, the reader misses a sense of restraint both in the matter and in the manner of the Divan. To many Persians, Hafiz occupies the place that is filled by Shakespeare in the minds of many Englishmen. It may be a national prejudice, but I cannot bring myself to believe that the mental food supplied by the Oriental is as good as the other. But, then, our appetites are not the same.

The tendency in dealing with a mystical poet is to read into him so-called deeper meanings, even when the simple meaning is clear enough and sufficient in itself. Hafiz is one of those who has suffered from this process ; it has removed him, in great measure, from the touch of human sympathies which are, when all is said and done, a poet's true kingdom. Of a different age, a different race, and a different civilisation from ours, there are yet snatches in his songs of that melody of human life which is everywhere the same. When he cries, "My beloved is gone and I had not even bidden him farewell!" his words are as poignant now as they were five centuries ago, and they could gain nothing from a mystical interpretation. As simple and as touching is his lament for his son: "Alas! he found it easy to depart, but unto me he left the harder pilgrimage." And for his wife: "Then said my heart, I will rest me in this city which is illumined by her presence; already her feet were bent upon a longer journey, but my poor heart knew it not." Not Shakespeare himself has found a more passionate image for love than; "Open my grave when I am dead, and thou shalt see a cloud of smoke rising out from it; then shalt thou know that the fire still burns in my dead heart—yea, it has set my very winding-sheet alight." Or: "If the scent of her hair were to blow across my dust when I had been dead a hundred years, my mouldering bones would rise and come dancing out of the tomb." And he knows of what he writes when he says, "I have estimated the influence of Reason upon Love and found that it is like that of a raindrop upon the ocean, which makes one little mark upon the water's face and disappears." These are the utterances of a great poet, the imaginative interpreter of the heart of man; they are not of one age, or of another, but for all time. Fitz-Gerald knew it when he declared that Hafiz rang true. " Hafiz is the most Persian of the Persians," he says. " He is the best representative of their character, whether his Saki and wine be real or mystical. Their religion and philosophy is soon seen through, and always seems to me cuckooed over like a borrowed thing, which people once having got do not know how to parade enough. To be sure their roses and nightingales are repeated often enough. But Hafiz and old Omar Khayyam ring like true metal." The criticism and the praise seem to me both just and delicate.

To a certain extent it may be said that the Sufiism of Hafiz is partly due to the natural leaning of the Oriental poet towards a picturesque diction (for all poetry must, to satisfy Eastern readers, be couched in a veiled and enigmatic speech),[1]

[1] Listen to the advice of an Afghan singer who wrote his *Ars Poetica* in the mountains south of Peshawar about the middle of the seventeenth century :—

" The arrow needs an archer, and poetry a magician.

" He must hold ever in the hand of his mind the weighing scales of metre, rejecting the verse which is too short and that which is too long.

" His mistress, Truth, shall mount her black steed, the veil of allegory drawn across her brow.

" Let her shoot from beneath her eyelashes a hundred glances, challenging and victorious.

" Let the poet place upon her fingers the jewels of the art of many hues, adorn her with the sandal-wood and the saffron of metaphor ;

" The bells of alliteration like bangles upon her feet, and on her bosom the necklace of a mysterious rhythm.

" Add to these the hidden meaning, like eyes half seen

and has partly been read into the Divan by later ages. But this is not all. With Shah Shudja, I would accuse him of mixing up inextricably wine and love and Sufi teaching, and perhaps more besides. To some at least of the innumerable difficulties which assail every man who turns a thoughtful eye upon life and its conditions, Hafiz seems to have accepted the solution presented to him by Sufiism. He understood and sympathised with the bold heresy of Hallaj, " though fools whom God hath not uplifted know not the meaning of him who said, I am God." Sometimes we find him enunciating one of the abstruser of the Sufi doctrines : " How shall I say that existence is mine when I have no knowledge of myself, or how that I exist not when mine eyes are fixed upon Him ? " —a man, that is, can lay claim to no individual existence ; all that he knows is that he is a part of the eternally existing. Or, again, he declares that his words are metaphorical, and should receive the full Sufi interpretation, as in the following couplet : " Boon companion, minstrel, and cup-bearer, all these are but names for Him ; the image of water

through their lashes, that her whole body may be a perfect mystery."—" *Translation of the Kilidi Afghani,*" *by T. C. Plowden.*

I fear the outcome of these directions is too often " amphora coepit institui, currente rota cur urceus exit," and perhaps the advice of Horace may be the better of the two " denique sit quod vis, simplex dumtaxat et unum."

and clay (man) is an illusion upon the road of life." But he handles Sufiism in a broad and noble manner, which links it on to the highest codes of morality accepted among the civilised races of mankind. "For all eternity the perfume of love comes not to him who has not swept with his cheek the dust from the tavern threshold"—"Blessed are the poor in spirit," Hafiz is saying in phraseology suited to the ears of those whom he addressed. "If thou desire the jewelled cup of ruby wine," he continues (and it is of the hunger and thirst after wisdom that he speaks), "ah, many tears shall thine eyes thread upon thine eyelashes!" He did not forget that "the Sufi gold is not always without alloy," and he was not one of those who believe that they have discovered the answer to all human demands when their own heart is satisfied. "Since thou canst never leave the palace of thyself," he warns us, "how canst thou hope to reach the village of truth." The song that filled his soul with gladness might strike on other ears to a different measure; and "where is the music to which both the drunk and the sober can dance?" He was, indeed, profoundly sceptical as to the infallibility of any creed, judging men not by the practice, but by the spirit that lay beneath it: "None shall die whose heart has lived with the life love breathed into it; but when the day of reckoning comes, I fancy that the Sheikh will find that he has gained as little by his abstinence as I by my feasting."

Sufiism apart, an undercurrent of mysticism runs through the poems which it is impossible to explain away. If we should attempt to ignore it, many of the odes would have no meaning at all, and most of them would lose a good half of their interest. Take, for instance, such verses as the following: "Heart and soul are fixed upon the desire of the Beloved: this at least *is*, for if not, heart and soul are nought. Fate is that which comes to the brink without the heart's blood; if not, all thy striving after the Garden of Paradise is nought. Throw thyself not at the foot of its sacred trees hoping for their shade; dost thou not see, oh cypress, that even these are nought unto thee?" Hafiz is engaged in that terrible weighing of possibilities which every man who thinks must know: "Surely the soul which is filled with the desire of God must have some quality which shall be stronger than death? But if this were not so . . . then indeed the soul itself is nought. Surely Fate is like an empty bowl standing upon the edge of the river of life? But if the bowl had been already filled with blood . . . then all your striving to reach the Garden of Paradise shall avail you nothing. For do you not see, you who dare to acknowledge the truth, that you cannot battle against an appointed

Destiny, and however grateful may be the shade of the holy trees, they could afford you no protection." Nor can I believe that it is an earthly love of whom he speaks when he says, " Since the Beloved has veiled his face, how comes it that his lovers are reciting his beauties ? They can only tell what they imagine to be there." We are all engaged in telling each other—only what we imagine to be there.

It is a curious coincidence (if it be nothing more) that at the time when mystical poetry was taking a recognised place in the literature of Persia and of India, it was also springing into existence in the West. The songs of the Troubadours were avowedly intended to convey a meaning deeper than that which lay upon the surface ; the Romance of the Rose comes nearer than any other Western allegory to a full-fledged mysticism worthy of an Oriental poet. St. Francis addresses his Redeemer in terms not very different from those used by Hafiz to express his longing after divine wisdom, and the Beatrice, perhaps of the *Vita Nuova*, certainly of the Divine Comedy, is no less intangible than the allegorical mistress (when she is allegorical) of the Persian.

Hafiz and Dante, it is interesting to note, were almost contemporaries. At the time when Dante was climbing Can Grande's weary stair, Hafiz was opening his eyes upon a yet more tumultuous world.

Both were driven by the confusion around them to look for some solid platform on which to build a theory of existence, but Dante found it in that strenuous personal faith which is for ever impossible to minds of the temper of that of Hafiz. Moreover, the mysticism of Dante stands with its feet planted firmly upon the earth : man and his deeds might be fleeting, but they laid so strong a hold upon the poet's imagination that he welded them into a stepping-stone to that which shall not pass away. His own life was spent in a ceaseless political activity ; for all his visionary journeys through heaven and hell, Dante lived as keenly as any of his contemporaries. The fire still burns in the dead heart ; the fierce and tender spirit, roused by turns to merciless condemnation and exquisite pity, still glows with a flame removed from mortal conditions, which the chill of death cannot extinguish as long as men shall read and understand. Through him his age lives. The people whom he had met, those of whom he had only heard, the smallest incidents of his time, the sum of all that it knew and of all that it believed, are struck out for ever, hard and sharp, in his vivid lines ; and the fortunes of Florence, of one little town in a little corner of the world, loom to us, under the poet's influence, as big and as tragic as they seemed to that most ardent of citizens. To Hafiz, on the contrary, modern instances have no value ; contemporary history is too small an episode to occupy his thoughts. During his lifetime the city that he loved, perhaps as dearly as Dante loved Florence, was besieged and taken five or six times ; it changed hands even more often. It was drenched with blood by one conqueror, filled with revelry by a second, and subjected to the hard rule of asceticism by a third. One after another Hafiz saw kings and princes rise into power and vanish " like snow upon the desert's dusty face." Pitiful tragedies, great rejoicings, the fall of kingdoms, and the clash of battle—all these he must have seen and heard. But what echo of them is there in his poems ? Almost none. An occasional allusion which learned commentators refer to some political event ; an exaggerated effusion in praise first of one king, then of another ; the celebration of such and such a victory and of the prowess of such and such a royal general—just what any self-respecting court poet would feel it incumbent upon himself to write ; and no more.

But some of us will feel that the apparent indifference of Hafiz lends to his philosophy a quality which that of Dante does not possess. The Italian is bound down within the limits of his own realism, his theory of the universe is essentially of his own age, and what to him was so acutely real is to many of us merely a beautiful or a terrible image. The picture that Hafiz drew represents a wider landscape, though the immediate foreground may not be so distinct. It is as if his mental eye, endowed with wonderful acuteness of vision, had penetrated into those provinces of thought which we of a later age were destined to inhabit. We can forgive him for leaving to us so indistinct a representation of his own time, and of the life of the individual in it, when we find him formulating ideas as profound as the warning that there is no musician to whose music both the drunk and the sober can dance.

Renan has put into a few luminous sentences his view of the mystical poets of India and Persia. " On sait que dans ces pays," he says, " s'est développée une vaste littérature où l'amour divin et l'amour terrestre se croisent d'une façon souvent difficile à démêler. L'origine de ce singulier genre de poésie est une question qui n'est pas encore éclaircie. Dans beaucoup de cas les sens mystiques prêtés à certaines poésies érotiques persanes et hindoues n'ont pas plus de réalité que les allégories du Cantique des Cantiques. Pour Hafiz, par exemple, il semble bien que l'explication allégorique est le plus souvent un fruit de la fantaisie des commentateurs, ou des précautions que les admirateurs du poète étaient obligés de prendre pour sauver l'orthodoxie de leur auteur favori. Puis l'imagination étant montée sur ce thème, et les esprits étant faussés par une exégèse qui ne voulait voir partout qu'allégories, on en est venu à faire des poèmes réellement à double sens. Comme ceux de Djellaleddin Rumi, de Wali, &c. . . . Dans l'Inde et la Perse ce genre de poésie (érotico-mystique) est le fruit d'un extrême raffinement, d'une imagination vive et portée au quiétisme, d'un certain goût du mystère, et aussi, en Perse du moins, de l'hypocrisie imposée par le fanatisme musulman. C'est, en effet, comme réaction contre la sécheresse de l'Islamisme que le soufisme a fait fortune chez les musulmans non arabes. Il y faut voir une révolte de l'esprit arien contre l'effroyante simplicité de l'esprit sémitique, excluant par la rigueur de sa théologie toute devotion particulière, toute doctrine secrète, toute combinaison religieuse vivante et variée." [1]

Those who have written poems " réellement à double sens " are careful to insist upon the mighty secrets that their words convey. " The things which wise men, who are sometimes called drunkards and sometimes seers," says one of them, " wish to express by the words wine, cup and cup-bearer, musician, magian, and Christian girdle, are so many profound mysteries which sometimes they translate by an enigma and sometimes they reveal." The symbols used by each writer are more or less the same ; there

[1] *Cantique des Cantiques*.

is an accepted Sufi code with which the initiated are acquainted. "The nightingale, and none beside, knows the full worth of the rose," sings Hafiz, "for many a one reads the leaf and understands not the meaning thereof." But though we may not all be nightingales, we have some guide to the interpretation of the leaf. Many of the words in the Sufi dictionary have been expounded to the outer world. The tavern, for instance, is the place of instruction or worship, of which the tavern-keeper is the teacher or priest, and the wine the spirit of divine knowledge which is poured out for his disciples; the idol is God; beauty is the divine perfection; shining locks the expansion of his glory; down on the cheek denotes the cloud of spirits that encircles his throne; and a black mole is the point of indivisible unity. The catalogue might be continued to any extent; almost every word has a vague and somewhat shifting significance in the language of mysticism, which he who has a mind for such exercises may decipher if he choose.

Hafiz is rather the forerunner than the founder of this school of poets. It is equally unsatisfactory to give a completely mystical or a completely material interpretation to his songs. He wrote of the world as he found it. In his experience pleasure and religion were the two most important incentives to human action; he ignored neither the one nor the other. I am very conscious that my appreciation of the poet is that of the Western. Exactly on what grounds he is appreciated in the East it is difficult to determine, and what his compatriots make of his teaching it is perhaps impossible to understand. From our point of view, then, the sum of his philosophy seems to be, that though there is little of which we can be certain, that little must always be the object of all men's desire ; each of us will set out upon the search for it along a different road, and if none will find his road easy to follow, each may, if he be wise, discover compensations for his toil by the wayside. And for the rest, " Who knows the secret of the veil ? " Like many a good and brave man before his time and since, I think he was content to " faintly trust the larger hope."

FROM THE DIVAN OF HAFIZ

F 2

POEMS FROM THE
DIVAN OF HAFIZ

I

ARISE, oh Cup-bearer, rise ! and bring
To lips that are thirsting the bowl they praise,
For it seemed that love was an easy thing,
But my feet have fallen on difficult ways.
I have prayed the wind o'er my heart to fling
The fragrance of musk in her hair that sleeps—
In the night of her hair—yet no fragrance stays
The tears of my heart's blood my sad heart weeps.

Hear the Tavern-keeper who counsels you :
" With wine, with red wine your prayer carpet dye ! "
There was never a traveller like him but knew
The ways of the road and the hostelry.
Where shall I rest, when the still night through,
Beyond thy gateway, oh Heart of my heart,
The bells of the camels lament and cry :
" Bind up thy burden again and depart ! "

The waves run high, night is clouded with fears,
And eddying whirlpools clash and roar ;

How shall my drowning voice strike their ears
Whose light-freighted vessels have reached the shore ?
I sought mine own ; the unsparing years
Have brought me mine own, a dishonoured name.
What cloak shall cover my misery o'er
When each jesting mouth has rehearsed my shame !

Oh Hafiz, seeking an end to strife,
Hold fast in thy mind what the wise have writ :
" If at last thou attain the desire of thy life,
Cast the world aside, yea, abandon it ! "

II

THE bird of gardens sang unto the rose,
New blown in the clear dawn : " Bow down thy head !
As fair as thou within this garden close,
Many have bloomed and died." She laughed and said :
" That I am born to fade grieves not my heart ;
But never was it a true lover's part
To vex with bitter words his love's repose."

The tavern step shall be thy hostelry,
For Love's diviner breath comes but to those
That suppliant on the dusty threshold lie.
And thou, if thou would'st drink the wine that flows
From Life's bejewelled goblet, ruby red,
Upon thine eyelashes thine eyes shall thread
A thousand tears for this temerity.

Last night when Irem's magic garden slept,
Stirring the hyacinth's purple tresses curled,
The wind of morning through the alleys stept.
" Where is thy cup, the mirror of the world ?
Ah, where is Love, thou Throne of Djem ? " I cried.
The breezes knew not ; but " Alas," they sighed,
" That happiness should sleep so long ! " and wept.

Not on the lips of men Love's secret lies,
Remote and unrevealed his dwelling-place.
Oh Saki, come ! the idle laughter dies
When thou the feast with heavenly wine dost grace.
Patience and wisdom, Hafiz, in a sea
Of thine own tears are drowned ; thy misery
They could not still nor hide from curious eyes.

III

WIND from the east, oh Lapwing of the day,
I send thee to my Lady, though the way
Is far to Saba, where I bid thee fly ;
Lest in the dust thy tameless wings should lie,
Broken with grief, I send thee to thy nest,
Fidelity.

Or far or near there is no halting-place
Upon Love's road—absent, I see thy face,

And in thine ear my wind-blown greetings sound,
North winds and east waft them where they are bound,
Each morn and eve convoys of greeting fair
I send to thee.

Unto mine eyes a stranger, thou that art
A comrade ever-present to my heart,
What whispered prayers and what full meed of praise
I send to thee.

Lest Sorrow's army waste thy heart's domain,
I send my life to bring thee peace again,
Dear life thy ransom ! From thy singers learn
How one that longs for thee may weep and burn ;
Sonnets and broken words, sweet notes and songs
I send to thee.

Give me the cup ! a voice rings in mine ears
Crying : " Bear patiently the bitter years !
For all thine ills, I send thee heavenly grace.
God the Creator mirrored in thy face
Thine eyes shall see, God's image in the glass
I send to thee.

" Hafiz, thy praise alone my comrades sing ;
Hasten to us, thou that art sorrowing !
A robe of honour and a harnessed steed
I send to thee."

IV

SLEEP on thine eyes, bright as narcissus flowers,
Falls not in vain!
And not in vain thy hair's soft radiance showers—
Ah, not in vain!

Before the milk upon thy lips was dry,
I said: "Lips where the salt of wit doth lie,
Sweets shall be mingled with thy mockery,
And not in vain!"

Thy mouth the fountain where Life's waters flow,
A dimpled well of tears is set below,
And death lies near to life thy lovers know,
But know in vain!

God send to thee great length of happy days!
Lo, not for his own life thy servant prays;
Love's dart in thy bent brows the Archer lays,
Nor shoots in vain.

Art thou with grief afflicted, with the smart
Of absence, and is bitter toil thy part?
Thy lamentations and thy tears, oh Heart,
Are not in vain!

Last night the wind from out her village blew,
And wandered all the garden alleys through,
Oh rose, tearing thy bosom's robe in two ;
'Twas not in vain !

And Hafiz, though thy heart within thee dies,
Hiding love's agony from curious eyes,
Ah, not in vain thy tears, not vain thy sighs,
Not all in vain !

V

Oh Turkish maid of Shiraz ! in thy hand
If thou'lt take my heart, for the mole on thy cheek
I would barter Bokhara and Samarkand.
Bring, Cup-bearer, all that is left of thy wine !
In the Garden of Paradise vainly thou'lt seek
The lip of the fountain of Ruknabad,
And the bowers of Mosalla where roses twine.

They have filled the city with blood and broil,
Those soft-voiced Lulis for whom we sigh ;
As Turkish robbers fall on the spoil,
They have robbed and plundered the peace of my heart.
Dowered is my mistress, a beggar am I ;
What shall I bring her ? a beautiful face
Needs nor jewel nor mole nor the tiring-maid's art.

Brave tales of singers and wine relate,
The key to the Hidden 'twere vain to seek ;
No wisdom of ours has unlocked that gate,
And locked to our wisdom it still shall be.
But of Joseph's beauty the lute shall speak ;
And the minstrel knows that Zuleika came forth,
Love parting the curtains of modesty.

When thou spokest ill of thy servant 'twas well—
God pardon thee ! for thy words were sweet ;
Not unwelcomed the bitterest answer fell
From lips where the ruby and sugar lay.
But, fair Love, let good counsel direct thy feet ;
Far dearer to youth than dear life itself
Are the warnings of one grown wise—and grey !

The song is sung and the pearl is strung ;
Come hither, oh Hafiz, and sing again !
And the listening Heavens above thee hung
Shall loose o'er thy verse the Pleiades' chain.

VI

A FLOWER-TINTED cheek, the flowery close
Of the fair earth, these are enough for me—
Enough that in the meadow wanes and grows
The shadow of a graceful cypress-tree.
I am no lover of hypocrisy ;

Of all the treasures that the earth can boast,
A brimming cup of wine I prize the most—
This is enough for me !

To them that here renowned for virtue live,
A heavenly palace is the meet reward ;
To me, the drunkard and the beggar, give
The temple of the grape with red wine stored !
Beside a river seat thee on the sward ;
It floweth past—so flows thy life away,
So sweetly, swiftly, fleets our little day—
Swift, but enough for me !

Look upon all the gold in the world's mart,
On all the tears the world hath shed in vain ;
Shall they not satisfy thy craving heart ?
I have enough of loss, enough of gain ;
I have my Love, what more can I obtain ?
Mine is the joy of her companionship
Whose healing lip is laid upon my lip—
This is enough for me !

I pray thee send not forth my naked soul
From its poor house to seek for Paradise ;
Though heaven and earth before me God unroll,
Back to thy village still my spirit flies.
And, Hafiz, at the door of Kismet lies
No just complaint—a mind like water clear,
A song that swells and dies upon the ear,
These are enough for thee !

DIVAN OF HAFIZ

VII

FROM the garden of Heaven a western breeze
Blows through the leaves of my garden of earth ;
With a love like a huri I'ld take mine ease,
And wine ! bring me wine, the giver of mirth !
To-day the beggar may boast him a king,
His banqueting-hall is the ripening field,
And his tent the shadow that soft clouds fling.

A tale of April the meadows unfold—
Ah, foolish for future credit to slave,
And to leave the cash of the present untold !
Build a fort with wine where thy heart may brave
The assault of the world ; when thy fortress falls,
The relentless victor shall knead from thy dust
The bricks that repair its crumbling walls.

Trust not the word of that foe in the fight !
Shall the lamp of the synagogue lend its flame
To set thy monastic torches alight ?
Drunken am I, yet place not my name
In the Book of Doom, nor pass judgment on it ;
Who knows what the secret finger of Fate
Upon his own white forehead has writ !

And when the spirit of Hafiz has fled,
Follow his bier with a tribute of sighs ;
Though the ocean of sin has closed o'er his head,
He may find a place in God's Paradise.

VIII

THE rose has flushed red, the bud has burst,
And drunk with joy is the nightingale—
Hail, Sufis! lovers of wine, all hail!
For wine is proclaimed to a world athirst.
Like a rock your repentance seemed to you;
Behold the marvel! of what avail
Was your rock, for a goblet has cleft it in two!

Bring wine for the king and the slave at the gate!
Alike for all is the banquet spread,
And drunk and sober are warmed and fed.
When the feast is done and the night grows late,
And the second door of the tavern gapes wide,
The low and the mighty must bow the head
'Neath the archway of Life, to meet what . . . outside?

Except thy road through affliction pass,
None may reach the halting-station of mirth;
God's treaty: Am I not Lord of the earth?
Man sealed with a sigh: Ah yes, alas!
Nor with Is nor Is Not let thy mind contend;
Rest assured all perfection of mortal birth
In the great Is Not at the last shall end.

For Assaf's pomp, and the steeds of the wind,
And the speech of birds, down the wind have fled,

And he that was lord of them all is dead;
Of his mastery nothing remains behind.
Shoot not thy feathered arrow astray!
A bow-shot's length through the air it has sped,
And then . . . dropped down in the dusty way.

But to thee, oh Hafiz, to thee, oh Tongue
That speaks through the mouth of the slender reed,
What thanks to thee when thy verses speed
From lip to lip, and the song thou hast sung?

IX

Oh Cup-bearer, set my glass afire
With the light of wine! oh minstrel, sing:
The world fulfilleth my heart's desire!
Reflected within the goblet's ring
I see the glow of my Love's red cheek,
And scant of wit, ye who fail to seek
The pleasures that wine alone can bring!

Let not the blandishments be checked
That slender beauties lavish on me,
Until in the grace of the cypress decked,
My Love shall come like a ruddy pine-tree
He cannot perish whose heart doth hold
The life love breathes—though my days are told,
In the Book of the World lives my constancy.

But when the Day of Reckoning is here,
I fancy little will be the gain
That accrues to the Sheikh for his lawful cheer,
Or to me for the draught forbidden I drain.
The drunken eyes of my comrades shine,
And I too, stretching my hand to the wine,
On the neck of drunkenness loosen the rein.

Oh wind, if thou passest the garden close
Of my heart's dear master, carry for me
The message I send to him, wind that blows!
" Why hast thou thrust from thy memory
My hapless name ? " breathe low in his ear ;
" Knowest thou not that the day is near
When nor thou nor any shall think on me ? "

If with tears, oh Hafiz, thine eyes are wet,
Scatter them round thee like grain, and snare
The Bird of Joy when it comes to thy net.
As the tulip shrinks from the cold night air,
So shrank my heart and quailed in the shade ;
Oh Song-bird Fortune, the toils are laid,
When shall thy bright wings lie pinioned there ?

The heavens' green sea and the bark therein,
The slender bark of the crescent moon,
Are lost in thy bounty's radiant noon,
Vizir and pilgrim, Kawameddin !

DIVAN OF HAFIZ

X

SINGER, sweet Singer, fresh notes strew,
Fresh and afresh and new and new!
Heart-gladdening wine thy lips imbrue,
Fresh and afresh and new and new!

Saki, thy radiant feet I hail;
Flush with red wine the goblets pale,
Flush our pale cheeks to drunken hue,
Fresh and afresh and new and new!

Then with thy love to toy with thee,
Rest thee, ah, rest! where none can see;
Seek thy delight, for kisses sue,
Fresh and afresh and new and new!

Here round thy life the vine is twined;
Drink! for elsewhere what wine wilt find?
Drink to her name, to hours that flew,
Hours ever fresh and new and new!

She that has stolen my heart from me,
How does she wield her empery?
Paints and adorns and scents her too,
Fresh and afresh and new and new!

Wind of the dawn that passest by,
Swift to the street of my fairy hie,
Whisper the tale of Hafiz true,
Fresh and afresh and new and new!

XI

MIRTH, Spring, to linger in a garden fair,
What more has earth to give? All ye that wait,
Where is the Cup-bearer, the flagon where?
When pleasant hours slip from the hand of Fate,
Reckon each hour as a certain gain;
Who seeks to know the end of mortal care
Shall question his experience in vain.

Thy fettered life hangs on a single thread—
Some comfort for thy present ills devise,
But those that time may bring thou shalt not dread.
Waters of Life and Irem's Paradise—
What meaning do our dreams and pomp convey,
Save that beside a mighty stream, wide-fed,
We sit and sing of wine and go our way!

The modest and the merry shall be seen
To boast their kinship with a single voice;
There are no differences to choose between,
Thou art but flattering thy soul with choice!

Who knows the Curtain's secret ? . . . Heaven is mute
And yet with Him who holds the Curtain, e'en
With Him, oh Braggart, thou would'st raise dispute !

Although His thrall shall miss the road and err,
'Tis but to teach him wisdom through distress,
Else Pardon and Compassionate Mercy were
But empty syllables and meaningless.
The Zealot thirsts for draughts of Kausar's wine,
And Hafiz doth an earthly cup prefer—
But what, between the two, is God's design ?

XII

WHERE is my ruined life, and where the fame
Of noble deeds ?
Look on my long-drawn road, and whence it came,
And where it leads !

Can drunkenness be linked to piety
And good repute ?
Where is the preacher's holy monody,
Where is the lute ?

From monkish cell and lying garb released,
Oh heart of mine,
Where is the Tavern fane, the Tavern priest,
Where is the wine ?

Past days of meeting, let the memory
Of you be sweet !
Where are those glances fled, and where for me
Reproaches meet ?

His friend's bright face warms not the enemy
When love is done—
Where is the extinguished lamp that made night day,
Where is the sun ?

Balm to mine eyes the dust, my head I bow
Upon thy stair.
Where shall I go, where from thy presence ? thou
Art everywhere.

Look not upon the dimple of her chin,
Danger lurks there !
Where wilt thou hide, oh trembling heart, fleeing in
Such mad haste—where ?

To steadfastness and patience, friend, ask not
If Hafiz keep—
Patience and steadfastness I have forgot,
And where is sleep ?

XIII

LADY that hast my heart within thy hand,
Thou heed'st me not ; and if thou turn thine ear
Unto the wise, thou shalt not understand—
Behold the fault is thine, our words were clear.

For all the tumult in my drunken brain
Praise God ! who trieth not His slave in vain ;
Nor this world nor the next shall make me fear !

My weary heart eternal silence keeps—
I know not who has slipped into my heart ;
Though I am silent, one within me weeps.
My soul shall rend the painted veil apart.
Where art thou, Minstrel ! touch thy saddest strings
Till clothed in music such as sorrow sings,
My mournful story from thy zither sweeps.

Lo, not at any time I lent mine ear
To hearken to the glories of the earth ;
Only thy beauty to mine eyes was dear.
Sleep has forsaken me, and from the birth
Of night till day I weave bright dreams of thee ;
Drunk with a hundred nights of revelry,
Where is the tavern that sets forth such cheer !

My heart, sad hermit, stains the cloister floor
With drops of blood, the sweat of anguish dire ;
Ah, wash me clean, and o'er my body pour
Love's generous wine ! the worshippers of fire
Have bowed them down and magnified my name,
For in my heart there burns a living flame,
Transpiercing Death's impenetrable door.

What instrument through last night's silence rang ?
My life into his lay the minstrel wove,

And filled my brain with the sweet song he sang.
It was the proclamation of thy love
That shook the strings of Life's most secret lyre,
And still my breast heaves with last night's desire,
For countless echoes from that music sprang.

And ever, since the time that Hafiz heard
His Lady's voice, as from a rocky hill
Reverberates the softly spoken word,
So echoes of desire his bosom fill.

XIV

THE nightingale with drops of his heart's blood
Had nourished the red rose, then came a wind,
And catching at the boughs in envious mood,
A hundred thorns about his heart entwined.
Like to the parrot crunching sugar, good
Seemed the world to me who could not stay
The wind of Death that swept my hopes away.

Light of mine eyes and harvest of my heart,
And mine at least in changeless memory !
Ah, when he found it easy to depart,
He left the harder pilgrimage to me !
Oh Camel-driver, though the cordage start,
For God's sake help me lift my fallen load,
And Pity be my comrade of the road !

My face is seamed with dust, mine eyes are wet.
Of dust and tears the turquoise firmament
Kneadeth the bricks for joy's abode ; and yet . . .
Alas, and weeping yet I make lament !
Because the moon her jealous glances set
Upon the bow-bent eyebrows of my moon,
He sought a lodging in the grave—too soon !

I had not castled, and the time is gone.
What shall I play ? Upon the chequered floor
Of Night and Day, Death won the game—forlorn
And careless now, Hafiz can lose no more.

XV

Return ! that to a heart wounded full sore
Valiance and strength may enter in ; return !
And Life shall pause at the deserted door,
The cold dead body breathe again and burn.
Oh come ! and touch mine eyes, of thy sweet grace,
For I am blind to all but to thy face.
Open the gates and bid me see once more !

Like to a cruel Ethiopian band,
Sorrow despoiled the kingdom of my heart—
Return ! glad Lord of Rome, and free the land ;
Before thine arms the foe shall break and part.
See now, I hold a mirror to mine eyes,
And nought but thy reflection therein lies ;
The glass speaks truth to them that understand.

Night is with child, hast thou not heard men say ?
" Night is with child ! what will she bring to birth ? "
I sit and ask the stars when thou'rt away.
Oh come ! and when the nightingale of mirth
Pipes in the Spring-awakened garden ground,
In Hafiz' heart shall ring a sweeter sound,
Diviner nightingales attune their lay.

XVI

What is wrought in the forge of the living and life—
All things are nought ! Ho ! fill me the bowl,
For nought is the gear of the world and the strife !
One passion has quickened the heart and the soul,
The Beloved's presence alone they have sought—
Love at least exists ; yet if Love were not,
Heart and soul would sink to the common lot—
All things are nought !

Like an empty cup is the fate of each,
That each must fill from Life's mighty flood ;
Nought thy toil, though to Paradise gate thou reach,
If Another has filled up thy cup with blood ;
Neither shade from the sweet-fruited trees could be bought
By thy praying—oh Cypress of Truth, dost not see
That Sidreh and Tuba were nought, and to thee
All then were nought !

The span of thy life is as five little days,
Brief hours and swift in this halting-place ;
Rest softly, ah rest ! while the Shadow delays,
For Time's self is nought and the dial's face.
On the lip of Oblivion we linger, and short
Is the way from the Lip to the Mouth where we pass—
While the moment is thine, fill, oh Saki, the glass
Ere all is nought !

Consider the rose that breaks into flower,
Neither repines though she fade and die—
The powers of the world endure for an hour,
But nought shall remain of their majesty.
Be not too sure of your crown, you who thought
That virtue was easy and recompense yours ;
From the monastery to the wine-tavern doors
The way is nought

What though I, too, have tasted the salt of my tears,
Though I, too, have burnt in the fires of grief,
Shall I cry aloud to unheeding ears ?
Mourn and be silent ! nought brings relief.
Thou, Hafiz, art praised for the songs thou hast wrought,
But bearing a stained or an honoured name,
The lovers of wine shall make light of thy fame—
All things are nought !

XVII

LAY not reproach at the drunkard's door
Oh Fanatic, thou that art pure of soul ;
Not thine on the page of life to enrol
The faults of others ! Or less or more
I have swerved from my path—keep thou to thine own
For every man when he reaches the goal
Shall reap the harvest his hands have sown.

Leave me the hope of a former grace—
Till the curtain is lifted none can tell
Whether in Heaven or deepest Hell,
Fair or vile, shall appear his face.
Alike the drunk and the strict of fare
For his mistress yearns—in the mosque Love doth dwell
And the church, for his lodging is everywhere.

If without the house of devotion I stand,
I am not the first to throw wide the door ;
My father opened it long before,
The eternal Paradise slipped from his hand.
All you that misconstrue my words' intent,
I lie on the bricks of the tavern floor,
And a brick shall serve me for argument.

Heaven's garden future treasures may yield—
Ah, make the most of earth's treasury !

The flickering shade of the willow-tree,
And the grass-grown lip of the fruitful field.
Trust not in deeds—the Eternal Day
Shall reveal the Creator's sentence on thee;
But till then, what His finger has writ, who can say.

Bring the cup in thine hand to the Judgment-seat;
Thou shalt rise, oh Hafiz, to Heaven's gate
From the tavern where thou hast tarried late.
And if thou hast worshipped wine, thou shalt meet
The reward that the Faithful attain;
If such thy life, then fear not thy fate,
Thou shalt not have lived and worshipped in vain

XVIII

Slaves of thy shining eyes are even those
That diadems of might and empire bear;
Drunk with the wine that from thy red lip flows,
Are they that e'en the grape's delight forswear.
Drift, like the wind across a violet bed,
Before thy many lovers, weeping low,
And clad like violets in blue robes of woe,
Who feel thy wind-blown hair and bow the head.

Thy messenger the breath of dawn, and mine
A stream of tears, since lover and beloved
Keep not their secret; through my verses shine,
Though other lays my flower's grace have proved

And countless nightingales have sung thy praise.
When veiled beneath thy curls thou passest, see,
To right and leftward those that welcome thee
Have bartered peace and rest on thee to gaze!

But thou that knowest God by heart, away!
Wine-drunk, love-drunk, we inherit Paradise,
His mercy is for sinners; hence and pray
Where wine thy cheek red as red erghwan dyes,
And leave the cell to faces sinister.
Oh Khizr, whose happy feet bathed in life's fount,
Help one who toils afoot—the horsemen mount
And hasten on their way; I scarce can stir.

Ah, loose me not! ah, set not Hafiz free
From out the bondage of thy gleaming hair!
Safe only those, safe, and at liberty,
That fast enchained in thy linked ringlets are.
But from the image of his dusty cheek
Learn this from Hafiz: proudest heads shall bend,
And dwellers on the threshold of a friend
Be crownèd with the dust that crowns the meek.

XIX

WHAT drunkenness is this that brings me hope—
Who was the Cup-bearer, and whence the wine?
That minstrel singing with full voice divine,
What lay was his? for 'mid the woven rope
Of song, he brought word from my Friend to me
Set to his melody.

The wind itself bore joy to Solomon ;
The Lapwing flew from Sheba's garden close,
Bringing good tidings of its queen and rose.
Take thou the cup and go where meadows span
The plain, whither the bird with tuneful throat
Has brought Spring's sweeter note.

Welcome, oh rose, and full-blown eglantine !
The violets their scented gladness fling,
Jasmin breathes purity—art sorrowing
Like an unopened bud, oh heart of mine ?
The wind of dawn that sets closed blossoms free
Brings its warm airs to thee.

Saki, thy kiss shall still my bitter cry !
Lift up your grief-bowed heads, all ye that weep,
The Healer brings joy's wine-cup—oh, drink deep !
Disciple of the Tavern-priest am I ;
The pious Sheikh may promise future bliss,
He brings me where joy is.

The greedy glances of a Tartar horde
To me seemed kind—my foeman spared me not
Though one poor robe was all that I had got.
But Heaven served Hafiz, as a slave his lord,
And when he fled through regions desolate,
Heaven brought him to thy gate.

XX

FROM out the street of So-and-So,
Oh wind, bring perfumes sweet to me
For I am sick and pale with woe ;
Oh bring me rest from misery !
The dust that lies before her door,
Love's long desired elixir, pour
Upon this wasted heart of mine—
Bring me a promise and a sign !

Between the ambush of mine eyes
And my heart's fort there's enmity—
Her eye-brow's bow, the dart that flies,
Beneath her lashes, bring to me !
Sorrow and absence, glances cold,
Before my time have made me old ;
A wine-cup from the hand of Youth
Bring me for pity and for ruth !

Then shall all unbelievers taste
A draught or two of that same wine ;
But if they like it not, oh haste !
And let joy's flowing cup be mine.
Cup-bearer, seize to-day, nor wait
Until to-morrow !—or from Fate
Some passport to felicity,
Some written surety bring to me !

My heart threw back the veil of woe,
Consoled by Hafiz' melody :
From out the street of So-and-So,
Oh wind, bring perfumes sweet to me !

XXI

Not all the sum of earthly happiness
Is worth the bowed head of a moment's pain,
And if I sell for wine my dervish dress,
Worth more than what I sell is what I gain !
Land where my Lady dwells, thou holdest me
Enchained ; else Fars were but a barren soil,
Not worth the journey over land and sea,
Not worth the toil !

Down in the quarter where they sell red wine,
My holy carpet scarce would fetch a cup—
How brave a pledge of piety is mine,
Which is not worth a goblet foaming up !
Mine enemy heaped scorn on me and said :
" Forth from the tavern gate ! " Why am I thrust
From off the threshold ? is my fallen head
Not worth the dust ?

Wash white that travel-stained sad robe of thine !
Where word and deed alike one colour bear,
The grape's fair purple garment shall outshine
Thy many-coloured rags and tattered gear.

Full easy seemed the sorrow of the sea
Lightened by hope of gain—hope flew too fast !
A hundred pearls were poor indemnity,
Not worth the blast.

The Sultan's crown, with priceless jewels set,
Encircles fear of death and constant dread ;
It is a head-dress much desired—and yet
Art sure 'tis worth the danger to the head ?
'Twere best for thee to hide thy face from those
That long for thee ; the Conqueror's reward
Is never worth the army's long-drawn woes,
Worth fire and sword.

Ah, seek the treasure of a mind at rest
And store it in the treasury of Ease ;
Not worth a loyal heart, a tranquil breast,
Were all the riches of thy lands and seas !
Ah, scorn, like Hafiz, the delights of earth,
Ask not one grain of favour from the base,
Two hundred sacks of jewels were not worth
Thy soul's disgrace !

XXII

The rose is not fair without the beloved's face,
Nor merry the Spring without the sweet laughter of wine ;
The path through the fields, and winds from a flower-strewn place,

Without her bright cheek, which glows like a tulip
fine,
Nor winds softly blowing, fields deep in corn, are fair.

And lips like to sugar, grace like a flower that sways,
Are nought without kisses many and dalliance sweet ;
If thousands of voices sang not the rose's praise,
The joy of the cypress her opening bud to greet,
Nor dancing of boughs nor blossoming rose were fair.

Though limned by most skilful fingers, no pictures
please
Unless the beloved's image is drawn therein ;
The garden and flowers, and hair flowing loose on the
breeze,
Unless to my Lady's side I may strive and win,
Nor garden, nor flowers, nor loose flying curls are fair.

Hast seen at a marriage-feast, when the mirth runs high,
The revellers scatter gold with a careless hand ?
The gold of thy heart, oh Hafiz, despised doth lie,
Not worthy thy love to be cast by a drunken band
At the feet of her who is fairer than all that's fair.

XXIII

My lady, that did change this house of mine
Into a heaven when that she dwelt therein,
From head to foot an angel's grace divine
Enwrapped her ; pure she was, spotless of sin ;

Fair as the moon her countenance, and wise ;
Lords of the kind and tender glance, her eyes
With an abounding loveliness did shine.

Then said my heart : Here will I take my rest !
This city breathes her love in every part.
But to a distant bourne was she addressed,
Alas ! he knew it not, alas, poor heart !
The influence of some cold malignant star
Has loosed my hand that held her, lone and far
She journeyeth that lay upon my breast.

Not only did she lift my bosom's veil,
Reveal its inmost secret, but her grace
Drew back the curtain from Heaven's mansions pale,
And gave her there an eternal dwelling-place.
The flower-strewn river lip and meadows fair,
The rose herself but fleeting treasures were,
Regret and Winter follow in their trail.

Dear were the days which perished with my friend—
Ah, what is left of life, now she is dead,
All wisdomless and profitless I spend !
The nightingale his own life's blood doth shed,
When, to the kisses of the wind, the morn
Unveils the rose's splendour—with his torn
And jealous breast he dyes her petals red.

Yet pardon her, oh Heart, for poor wert thou,
A humble dervish on the dusty way ;

Crowned with the crown of empire was her brow,
And in the realms of beauty she bore sway.
But all the joy that Hafiz' hand might hold,
Lay in the beads that morn and eve he told,
Worn with God's praise; and see! he holds it now.

XXIV

Not one is filled with madness like to mine
In all the taverns! my soiled robe lies here,
There my neglected book, both pledged for wine.
With dust my heart is thick, that should be clear,
A glass to mirror forth the Great King's face;
One ray of light from out Thy dwelling-place
To pierce my night, oh God! and draw me near.

From out mine eyes unto my garment's hem
A river flows; perchance my cypress-tree
Beside that stream may rear her lofty stem,
Watering her roots with tears. Ah, bring to me
The wine vessel! since my Love's cheek is hid,
A flood of grief comes from my heart unbid,
And turns mine eyes into a bitter sea!

Nay, by the hand that sells me wine, I vow
No more the brimming cup shall touch my lips,
Until my mistress with her radiant brow
Adorns my feast—until Love's secret slips

From her, as from the candle's tongue of flame,
Though I, the singèd moth, for very shame,
Dare not extol Love's light without eclipse.

Red wine I worship, and I worship her !—
Speak not to me of anything beside,
For nought but these on earth or heaven I care.
What though the proud narcissus flowers defied
Thy shining eyes to prove themselves more bright,
Yet heed them not ! those that are clear of sight
Follow not them to whom all light's denied.

Before the tavern door a Christian sang
To sound of pipe and drum, what time the earth
Awaited the white dawn, and gaily rang
Upon mine ear those harbingers of mirth :
" If the True Faith be such as thou dost say,
Alas ! my Hafiz, that this sweet To-day
Should bring unknown To-morrow to the birth ! "

XXV

THE days of absence and the bitter nights
Of separation, all are at an end !
Where is the influence of the star that blights
My hope ? The omen answers : At an end !
Autumn's abundance, creeping Autumn's mirth,
Are ended and forgot when o'er the earth
The wind of Spring with soft warm feet doth wend.

The Day of Hope, hid beneath Sorrow's veil,
Has shown its face—ah, cry that all may hear :
Come forth ! the powers of night no more prevail !
Praise be to God, now that the rose is near
With long-desired and flaming coronet,
The cruel stinging thorns all men forget,
The wind of Winter ends its proud career.

The long confusion of the nights that were,
Anguish that dwelt within my heart, is o'er ;
'Neath the protection of my lady's hair
Grief nor disquiet come to me no more.
What though her curls wrought all my misery,
My lady's gracious face can comfort me,
And at the end give what I sorrow for.

Light-hearted to the tavern let me go,
Where laughs the pipe, the merry cymbals kiss;
Under the history of all my woe,
My mistress sets her hand and writes : Finis.
Oh, linger not, nor trust the inconstant days
That promised : Where thou art thy lady stays—
The tale of separation ends with this !

Joy's certain path, oh Saki, thou hast shown—
Long may thy cup be full, thy days be fair !
Trouble and sickness from my breast have flown,
Order and health thy wisdom marshals there.

Not one that numbered Hafiz' name among
The great—unnumbered were his tears, unsung ;
Praise him that sets an end to endless care !

XXVI

THE secret draught of wine and love repressed
Are joys foundationless—then come whate'er
May come, slave to the grape I stand confessed !
Unloose, oh friend, the knot of thy heart's care,
Despite the warning that the Heavens reveal !
For all his thought, never astronomer
That loosed the knot of Fate those Heavens conceal !

Not all the changes that thy days unfold
Shall rouse thy wonder ; Time's revolving sphere
Over a thousand lives like thine has rolled.
That cup within thy fingers, dost not hear
The voices of dead kings speak through the clay
Kobad, Bahman, Djemshid, their dust is here,
" Gently upon me set thy lips ! " they say.

What man can tell where Kaus and Kai have gone ?
Who knows where even now the restless wind
Scatters the dust of Djem's imperial throne ?
And where the tulip, following close behind
The feet of Spring, her scarlet chalice rears,

There Ferhad for the love of Shirin pined,
Dyeing the desert red with his heart's tears.

Bring, bring the cup ! drink we while yet we may
To our soul's ruin the forbidden draught ;
Perhaps a treasure-trove is hid away
Among those ruins where the wine has laughed !—
Perhaps the tulip knows the fickleness
Of Fortune's smile, for on her stalk's green shaft
She bears a wine-cup through the wilderness.

The murmuring stream of Ruknabad, the breeze
That blows from out Mosalla's fair pleasaunce,
Summon me back when I would seek heart's ease,
Travelling afar ; what though Love's countenance
Be turned full harsh and sorrowful on me,
I care not so that Time's unfriendly glance
Still from my Lady's beauty turned be.

Like Hafiz, drain the goblet cheerfully
While minstrels touch the lute and sweetly sing,
For all that makes thy heart rejoice in thee
Hangs of Life's single, slender, silken string.

XXVII

My friend has fled ! alas, my friend has fled,
And left me nought but tears and pain behind !

Like smoke above a flame caught by the wind,
So rose she from my breast and forth she sped.
Drunk with desire, I seized Love's cup divine,
But she that held it poured the bitter wine
Of Separation into it and fled.

The hunter she, and I the helpless prey ;
Wounded and sick, round me her toils she drew,
My heart into a sea of sorrow threw,
Bound up her camel loads and fled away.
Fain had I laid an ambush for her soul,
She saw and vanished, and the timid foal,
Good Fortune, slipped the rein and would not stay.

My heart was all too narrow for my woe,
And tears of blood my weeping eyes have shed,
A crimson stream across the desert sped,
Rising from out my sad heart's overflow.
She knew not what Love's meanest slave can tell :
" 'Tis sweet to serve ! " but threw me a Farewell,
Kissing my threshold, turned, and cried " I go ! "

In the clear dawn, before the east was red,
Before the rose had torn her veil in two,
A nightingale through Hafiz' garden flew,
Stayed but to fill its song with tears, and fled.

DIVAN OF HAFIZ

XXVIII

HAST thou forgotten when thy stolen glance
Was turned to me, when on my happy face
Clearly thy love was writ, which doth enhance
All happiness ? or when my sore disgrace
(Hast thou forgot ?) drew from thine eyes reproof,
And made thee hold thy sweet red lips aloof,
Dowered, like Jesus's breath, with healing grace ?

Hast thou forgotten how the glorious
Swift nights flew past, the cup of dawn brimmed high ?
My love and I alone, God favouring us !
And when she like a waning moon did lie,
And Sleep had drawn his coif about her brow,
Hast thou forgot ? Heaven's crescent moon would bow
The head, and in her service pace the sky !

Hast thou forgotten, when a sojourner
Within the tavern gates and drunk with wine,
I found Love's passionate wisdom hidden there,
Which in the mosque none even now divine ?
The goblet's carbuncle (hast thou forgot ?)
Laughed out aloud, and speech flew hot
And fast between thy ruby lips and mine !

Hast thou forgotten when thy cheek's dear torch
Lighted the beacon of desire in me,

And when my heart, like foolish moths that scorch
Their wings and yet return, turned all to thee ?
Within the banquet-hall of Good Repute
(Hast thou forgot ?) the wine's self-pressed my suit,
And filled the morn with drunken jollity !

Hast thou forgotten when thou laid'st aright
The uncut gems of Hafiz' inmost thought,
And side by side thy sweet care strung the bright
Array of verse on verse—hast thou forgot ?

XXIX

FROM Canaan Joseph shall return, whose face
A little time was hidden : weep no more—
Oh, weep no more ! in sorrow's dwelling-place
The roses yet shall spring from the bare floor !
And heart bowed down beneath a secret pain—
Oh stricken heart ! joy shall return again,
Peace to the love-tossed brain—oh, weep no more !

Oh, weep no more ! for once again Life's Spring
Shall throne her in the meadows green, and o'er
Her head the minstrel of the night shall fling
A canopy of rose leaves, score on score.
The secret of the world thou shalt not learn,
And yet behind the veil Love's fire may burn—
Weep'st thou ? let hope return and weep no more !

To-day may pass, to-morrow pass, before
The turning wheel give me my heart's desire ;
Heaven's self shall change, and turn not evermore
The universal wheel of Fate in ire.
Oh Pilgrim nearing Mecca's holy fane,
The thorny maghilan wounds thee in vain,
The desert blooms again—oh, weep no more !

What though the river of mortality
Round the unstable house of Life doth roar,
Weep not, oh heart, Noah shall pilot thee,
And guide thine ark to the desirèd shore !
The goal lies far, and perilous is thy road,
Yet every path leads to that same abode
Where thou shalt drop thy load—oh, weep no more !

Mine enemies have persecuted me,
My Love has turned and fled from out my door—
God counts our tears and knows our misery ;
Ah, weep not ! He has heard thy weeping sore.
And chained in poverty and plunged in night,
Oh Hafiz, take thy Koran and recite
Litanies infinite, and weep no more !

XXX

All hail, Shiraz, hail ! oh site without peer !
May God be the Watchman before thy gate,

That the feet of Misfortune enter not here !
Lest my Ruknabad be left desolate,
A hundred times, " God forbid ! " I pray ;
Its limpid stream where the shadows wait
Like the fount of Khizr giveth life for aye.

'Twixt Jafrabad and Mosalla's close
Flies the north wind laden with ambergris—
Oh, come to Shiraz when the north wind blows !
There abideth the angel Gabriel's peace
With him who is lord of its treasures ; the fame
Of the sugar of Egypt shall fade and cease,
For the breath of our beauties has put it to shame.

Oh wind that blows from the sun-rising,
What news of the maid with the drunken eyes,
What news of the lovely maid dost thou bring ?
Bid me not wake from my dream and arise,
In dreams I have rested my head at her feet—
When stillness unbroken around me lies,
The vision of her makes my solitude sweet.

If for wine the Cup-bearer pour forth my blood,
As the milk from a mother's bosom flows,
At his word let my heart yield its crimson flood.
But, Hafiz, Hafiz ! thou art of those
For ever fearing lest absence be near ;
For the days when thou held'st the Beloved close,
Why rise not thy thanks so that all may hear ?

XXXI

THE breath of Dawn's musk-strewing wind shall blow,
The ancient world shall turn to youth again,
And other wines from out Spring's chalice flow ;
Wine-red, the judas-tree shall set before
The pure white jessamine a brimming cup,
And wind flowers lift their scarlet chalice up
For the star-pale narcissus to adore.

The long-drawn tyranny of grief shall pass,
Parting shall end in meeting, the lament
Of the sad bird that sang " Alas, alas ! "
Shall reach the rose in her red-curtained tent.
Forth from the mosque ! the tavern calls to me !
Would'st hinder us ? The preacher's homily
Is long, but life will soon be spent !

Ah, foolish Heart ! the pleasures of To-day,
If thou abandon, will To-morrow stand
Thy surety for the gold thou'st thrown away ?
In Sha'aban the troops of Grief disband,
And crown the hours with wine's red coronet—
The sun of merriment ere long will set,
And meagre Ramazan is close at hand !

Dear is the rose—now, now her sweets proclaim,
While yet the purple petals blush and blow ;

Hither adown the path of Spring she came,
And by the path of Autumn she will go.
Now, while we listen, Minstrel, tune thy lay!
Thyself hast said: "The Present steals away;
The Future comes, and bringing—what? Dost know?"

Summoned by thy melody did Hafiz rise
Out of the darkness near thy lips to dwell;
Back to the dark again his pathway lies—
Sing out, sing clear, and singing cry: Farewell!

XXXII

Upon a branch of the straight cypress-tree
Once more the patient nightingale doth rest:
"Oh Rose!" he cries, "evil be turned from thee!
I sing thee all men's thanks; thou blossomest
And hope springs up in every joyless heart—
Let not the nightingale lament apart,
Nor with thy proud thorns wound his faithful breast."

I will not mourn my woeful banishment,
He that has hungered for his lady's face
Shall, when she cometh, know a great content.
The Zealot seeks a heavenly dwelling-place,
Huris to welcome him in Paradise;
Here at the tavern gate my heaven lies,
I need no welcome but my lady's grace.

Better to drink red wine than tears, say I,
While the lute sings ; and if one bid thee cease,
" God is the merciful ! " thou shalt reply.
To some, life brings but joy and endless ease ;
Ah, let them laugh although the jest be vain !
For me the source of pleasure lay in pain,
And weeping for my lady I found peace.

Hafiz, why art thou ever telling o'er
The tale of absence and of sorrow's night ?
Knowest thou not that parting goes before
All meeting, and from darkness comes the light !

XXXIII

THE jewel of the secret treasury
Is still the same as once it was ; the seal
Upon Love's treasure casket, and the key,
Are still what thieves can neither break nor steal ;
Still among lovers loyalty is found,
And therefore faithful eyes still strew the ground
With the same pearls that mine once strewed for thee.

Question the wandering winds and thou shalt know
That from the dusk until the dawn doth break,
My consolation is that still they blow
The perfume of thy curls across my cheek.
A dart from thy bent brows has wounded me—

Ah, come ! my heart still waiteth helplessly,
Has waited ever, till thou heal its pain.

If seekers after rubies there were none,
Still to the dark mines where the gems had lain
Would pierce, as he was wont, the radiant sun,
Setting the stones ablaze. Would'st hide the stain
Of my heart's blood ? Blood-red the ruby glows
(And whence it came my wounded bosom knows)
Upon thy lips to show what thou hast done.

Let not thy curls waylay my pilgrim soul,
As robbers use, and plunder me no more !
Years join dead year, but thine extortionate rule
Is still the same, merciless as before.
Sing, Hafiz, sing again of eyes that weep !
For still the fountain of our tears is deep
As once it was, and still with tears is full.

XXXIV

LAST night I dreamed that angels stood without
The tavern door, and knocked in vain, and wept ;
They took the clay of Adam, and, methought,
Moulded a cup therewith while all men slept.
Oh dwellers in the halls of Chastity !
You brought Love's passionate red wine to me,
Down to the dust I am, your bright feet stept.

For Heaven's self was all too weak to bear
The burden of His love God laid on it,
He turned to seek a messenger elsewhere,
And in the Book of Fate my name was writ.
Between my Lord and me such concord lies.
As makes the Huris glad in Paradise,
With songs of praise through the green glades they flit.

A hundred dreams of Fancy's garnered store
Assail me—Father Adam went astray
Tempted by one poor grain of corn ! Wherefore
Absolve and pardon him that turns away
Though the soft breath of Truth reaches his ears,
For two-and-seventy jangling creeds he hears,
And loud-voiced Fable calls him ceaselessly.

That, that is not the flame of Love's true fire
Which makes the torchlight shadows dance in rings,
But where the radiance draws the moth's desire
And send him forth with scorched and drooping wings.
The heart of one who dwells retired shall break,
Rememb'ring a black mole and a red cheek,
And his life ebb, sapped at its secret springs.

Yet since the earliest time that man has sought
To comb the locks of Speech, his goodly bride,
Not one, like Hafiz, from the face of Thought
Has torn the veil of Ignorance aside.

XXXV

Forget not when dear friend to friend returned,
Forget not days gone by, forget them not !
My mouth has tasted bitterness, and learned
To drink the envenomed cup of mortal lot ;
Forget not when a sweeter draught was mine,
Loud rose the songs of them that drank that wine—
Forget them not !

Forget not loyal lovers long since dead,
Though faith and loyalty should be forgot,
Though the earth cover the enamoured head,
And in the dust wisdom and passion rot.
My friends have thrust me from their memory ;
Vainly a thousand thousand times I cry :
Forget me not !

Weary I turn me to my bonds again.
Once there were hands strong to deliver me,
Forget not when they broke a poor slave's chain !
Though from mine eyes tears flow unceasingly,
I think on them whose rose gardens are set
Beside the Zindeh Rud, and I forget
Life's misery.

Sorrow has made her lair in my breast,
And undisturbed she lies—forget them not

That drove her forth like to a hunted beast!
Hafiz, thou and thy tears shall be forgot,
Lock fast the gates of thy sad heart! But those
That held the key to thine unspoken woes—
Forget them not!

XXXVI

Beloved, who has bid thee ask no more
How fares my life? to play the enemy
And ask not where he dwells that was thy friend?
Thou art the breath of mercy passing o'er
The whole wide world, and the offender I;
Ah, let the rift my tears have channelled end,
Question the past no more!

If thou would'st know the secret of Love's fire,
It shall be manifest unto thine eyes:
Question the torch flame burning steadfastly,
But ask no more the sweet wind's wayward choir.
Ask me of faith and love that never dies;
Darius, Alexander's sovereignty,
I sing of these no more.

Ask not the monk to give thee Truth's pure gold,
He hides no riches 'neath his lying guise;
And ask not him to teach thee alchemy
Whose treasure-house is bare, his hearth-stone cold.

Ask to what goal the wandering dervish hies,
They knew not his desire who counselled thee :
Question his rags no more !

And in their learned books thou'lt seek in vain
The key to Love's locked gateway ; Heart grown wise
In pain and sorrow, ask no remedy !
But when the time of roses comes again,
Take what it gives, oh Hafiz, ere it flies,
And ask not why the hour has brought it thee,
And wherefore ask no more !

XXXVII

ARISE ! and fill a golden goblet up
Until the wine of pleasure overflow,
Before into thy skull's pale empty cup
A grimmer Cup-bearer the dust shall throw.
Yea, to the Vale of Silence we must come ;
Yet shall the flagon laugh and Heaven's dome
Thrill with an answering echo ere we go !

Thou knowest that the riches of this field
Make no abiding, let the goblet's fire
Consume the fleeting harvest Earth may yield !
Oh Cypress-tree ! green home of Love's sweet choir,
When I unto the dust I am have passed,
Forget thy former wantonness, and cast
Thy shadow o'er the dust of my desire.

Flow, bitter tears, and wash me clean ! for they
Whose feet are set upon the road that lies
'Twixt Earth and Heaven : " Thou shalt be pure,"
    they say,
" Before unto the pure thou lift thine eyes."
Seeing but himself, the Zealot sees but sin ;
Grief to the mirror of his soul let in,
Oh Lord, and cloud it with the breath of sighs !

No tainted eye shall gaze upon her face,
No glass but that of an unsullied heart
Shall dare reflect my Lady's perfect grace.
Though like to snakes that from the herbage start,
Thy curling locks have wounded me full sore,
Thy red lips hold the power of the bezoar—
Ah, touch and heal me where I lie apart !

And when from her the wind blows perfume sweet,
Tear, Hafiz, like the rose, thy robe in two,
And cast thy rags beneath her flying feet,
To deck the place thy mistress passes through.

XXXVIII

I CEASE not from desire till my desire
Is satisfied ; or let my mouth attain
My love's red mouth, or let my soul expire,
Sighed from those lips that sought her lips in vain.

Others may find another love as fair ;
Upon her threshold I have laid my head,
The dust shall cover me, still lying there,
When from my body life and love have fled.

My soul is on my lips ready to fly,
But grief beats in my heart and will not cease,
Because not once, not once before I die,
Will her sweet lips give all my longing peace.
My breath is narrowed down to one long sigh
For a red mouth that burns my thoughts like fire ;
When will that mouth draw near and make reply
To one whose life is straitened with desire ?

When I am dead, open my grave and see
The cloud of smoke that rises round thy feet :
In my dead heart the fire still burns for thee ;
Yea, the smoke rises from my winding-sheet !
Ah, come, Beloved ! for the meadows wait
Thy coming, and the thorn bears flowers instead
Of thorns, the cypress fruit, and desolate
Bare winter from before thy steps has fled.

Hoping within some garden ground to find
A red rose soft and sweet as thy soft cheek,
Through every meadow blows the western wind,
Through every garden he is fain to seek.

Reveal thy face ! that the whole world may be
Bewildered by thy radiant loveliness ;
The cry of man and woman comes to thee,
Open thy lips and comfort their distress !

Each curling lock of thy luxuriant hair
Breaks into barbèd hooks to catch my heart,
My broken heart is wounded everywhere
With countless wounds from which the red drops start.
Yet when sad lovers meet and tell their sighs,
Not without praise shall Hafiz' name be said,
Not without tears, in those pale companies
Where joy has been forgot and hope has fled.

XXXIX

Cypress and Tulip and sweet Eglantine,
Of these the tale from lip to lip is sent ;
Washed by three cups, oh Saki, of thy wine,
My song shall turn upon this argument.
Spring, bride of all the meadows, rises up,
Clothed in her ripest beauty : fill the cup !
Of Spring's handmaidens runs this song of mine.

The sugar-loving birds of distant Ind,
Except a Persian sweetmeat that was brought

To fair Bengal, have found nought to their mind.
See how my song, that in one night was wrought,
Defies the limits set by space and time !
O'er plains and mountain-tops my fearless rhyme,
Child of a night, its year-long road shall find.

And thou whose sense is dimmed with piety,
Thou too shalt learn the magic of her eyes ;
Forth comes the caravan of sorcery
When from those gates the blue-veined curtains rise.
And when she walks the flowery meadows through,
Upon the jasmine's shamèd cheek the dew
Gathers like sweat, she is so fair to see !

Ah, swerve not from the path of righteousness
Though the world lure thee ! like a wrinkled crone,
Hiding beneath her robe lasciviousness,
She plunders them that pause and heed her moan.
From Sinai Moses brings thee wealth untold ;
Bow not thine head before the calf of gold
Like Samir, following after wickedness.

From the Shah's garden blows the wind of Spring,
The tulip in her lifted chalice bears
A dewy wine of Heaven's minist'ring ;
Until Ghiyasuddin, the Sultan, hears,
Sing, Hafiz, of thy longing for his face.

The breezes whispering round thy dwelling-place
Shall carry thy lament unto the King.

XL

THE margin of a stream, the willow's shade,
A mind inclined to song, a mistress sweet,
A Cup-bearer whose cheek outshines the rose,
A friend upon whose heart thy heart is laid :
Oh Happy-starred ! let not thine hours fleet
Unvalued ; may each minute as it goes
Lay tribute of enjoyment at thy feet,
That thou may'st live and know thy life is sweet.

Let every one upon whose heart desire
For a fair face lies like a burden sore,
That all his hopes may reach their goal unchecked,
Throw branches of wild rue upon his fire.
My soul is like a bride, with a rich store
Of maiden thoughts and jewelled fancies decked,
And in Time's gallery I yet may meet
Some picture meant for me, some image sweet.

Give thanks for nights spent in good company,
And take the gifts a tranquil mind may bring ;
No heart is dark when the kind moon doth shine,
And grass-grown river-banks are fair to see.

The Saki's radiant eyes, God favouring,
Are like a wine-cup brimming o'er with wine,
And him my drunken sense goes out to greet,
For e'en the pain he leaves behind is sweet.

Hafiz, thy life has sped untouched by care,
With me towards the tavern turn thy feet!
The fairest robbers thou'lt encounter there,
And they will teach thee what to learn is sweet.

XLI

THE days of Spring are here! the eglantine,
The rose, the tulip from the dust have risen—
And thou, why liest thou beneath the dust?
Like the full clouds of Spring, these eyes of mine
Shall scatter tears upon the grave thy prison,
Till thou too from the earth thine head shalt thrust.

XLII

TRUE love has vanished from every heart;
What has befallen all lovers fair?
When did the bonds of friendship part?—
What has befallen the friends that were?
Ah, why are the feet of Khizr lingering?—
The waters of life are no longer clear,

DIVAN OF HAFIZ

The purple rose has turned pale with fear,
And what has befallen the wind of Spring ?

None now sayeth : " A love was mine,
Loyal and wise, to dispel my care."
None remembers love's right divine ;
What has befallen all lovers fair ?
In the midst of the field, to the players' feet,
The ball of God's favour and mercy came,
But none has leapt forth to renew the game—
What has befallen the horsemen fleet ?

Roses have bloomed, yet no bird rejoiced,
No vibrating throat has rung with the tale ;
What can have silenced the hundred-voiced ?
What has befallen the nightingale ?
Heaven's music is hushed, and the planets roll
In silence ; has Zohra broken her lute ?
There is none to press out the vine's ripe fruit,
And what has befallen the foaming bowl ?

A city where kings are but lovers crowned,
A land from the dust of which friendship springs—
Who has laid waste that enchanted ground ?
What has befallen the city of kings ?
Years have passed since a ruby was won
From the mine of manhood ; they labour in vain,
The fleet-footed wind and the quickening rain,
And what has befallen the light of the sun ?

Hafiz, the secret of God's dread task
No man knoweth, in youth or prime
Or in wisest age ; of whom would'st thou ask :
What has befallen the wheels of Time ?

XLIII

WHERE are the tidings of union ? that I may arise—
Forth from the dust I will rise up to welcome thee !
My soul, like a homing bird, yearning for Paradise,
Shall arise and soar, from the snares of the world set free.
When the voice of thy love shall call me to be thy slave,
I shall rise to a greater far than the mastery
Of life and the living, time and the mortal span :
Pour down, oh Lord ! from the clouds of thy guiding grace.
The rain of a mercy that quickeneth on my grave,
Before, like dust that the wind bears from place to place,
I arise and flee beyond the knowledge of man.
When to my grave thou turnest thy blessed feet,
Wine and the lute thou shalt bring in thine hand to me,
Thy voice shall ring through the folds of my winding-sheet,
And I will arise and dance to thy minstrelsy.
Though I be old, clasp me one night to thy breast,
And I, when the dawn shall come to awaken me,
With the flush of youth on my cheek from thy bosom will rise.

DIVAN OF HAFIZ

Rise up! let mine eyes delight in thy stately grace!
Thou art the goal to which all men's endeavour has pressed,
And thou the idol of Hafiz' worship; thy face
From the world and life shall bid him come forth and arise!

NOTES

NOTES

I

Stanza 1.—The first line of this song, the opening poem in the Divan, is borrowed from an Arabic poem by Yezid ibn Moawiyah, the second Khalif of the Ommiad line. This prince was held in abomination by the Persian Shi'ites, both as the head of the Sunnis and because he was the cause of the death of Hussein, the son of Ali, whom the Shi'ites regarded as the rightful successor to the Khalifate. Hafiz was frequently reproached for setting a quotation from the works of the abhorred Yezid at the head of his book, a reproach which he is said to have met with the reply, that it was good policy to steal from the heretics whatsoever they possessed of worth.

" In this country (*i.e.* North-Eastern China) is found the best musk in the world, and I will tell you how it is produced. There exists in that region a kind of wild animal like a gazelle. It has feet and tail like the gazelle's, a stag's hair of a very coarse kind, but no horns. It has four tusks, two below and two above, about three inches long, and slender in form, one pair growing downwards and the other upwards. It is a very pretty creature. The musk is found in this way: when the creature has been taken, they find at the navel, between the flesh and the skin, something like an imposthume filled with blood, which they cut out and remove, with all the skin attached to it; and the blood inside this imposthume is the musk that produces that powerful perfume. There is an immense number of these beasts in the country we are speaking of. The flesh is very good to eat. Messer Marco brought the dried head and feet of one of these animals to Venice with him."—*Travels of Marco Polo*.

There is a play of meaning upon the musk which is obtained at the cost of the deer's life-blood and the tears of blood which the lover weeps for his mistress.

Stanza 2.—The title which Hafiz gives to the Tavern-keeper is Pir-i-Maghan—literally, the Old Man of the Magians. The history of this title is an epitome of the history of Persian faiths. It indicated primarily the priest of the first of Persian religions, that of Zoroaster. When the Mahommadans invaded Persia, and the preachers of the Prophet supplanted the priests of Zoroaster, their title fell into disrepute, and was degraded so far that it came to mean only the keeper of a tavern or caravanserai. But in this sense it gradually regained the honourable place from which it had fallen; for the keepers of such places of resort were, for the most part, men well acquainted with the "ways of the road and the hostelry." In their time they may themselves have served travellers upon their journey; they had heard and learnt much from the wayfarers who stopped at their gates, and they were able to guide others upon their journey, sending them forth refreshed and comforted in body. And here the Sufis took up the ancient name and used it to mean that wise old man who supplied weary travellers upon life's road with the spiritual draught of Sufi doctrine which refreshes and comforts the soul.

II

Stanza 1.—This poem has been expounded to me as a description of the poet's quest for love. In an allegory he shows how he looked for it in vain from that image of earthly devotion, the nightingale; he warns men that it comes not but by humiliation and sorrow; he questions the magic garden, but its breezes cannot answer him; finally, he concludes that love is not that which lies upon the lips of men, and calls upon the

Cup-bearer to silence their idle talk with the wine of divine knowledge.

Stanza 2.—The Garden of Irem was planted by the mythical King Shedad, the son of Ad, the grandson of Irem, who was himself the son of Shem. The tribe of Ad settled in the sandy deserts near Aden, where Ad began the building of a great city which his son completed. Round his palace Shedad planted a wonderful garden which was intended to rival in beauty the Garden of Eden. " When it was finished he set out with a great attendance to take a view of it, but when they were come within a day's journey of the place they were all destroyed by a terrible noise from heaven. . . . The city, they tell us, is still standing in the deserts of Aden, being preserved by Providence as a monument of divine justice, though it be invisible, unless very rarely, when God permits it to be seen, a favour one Colabah pretended to have received in the reign of the Khalif Moawiyah, who, sending for him to know the truth of the matter, Colabah related his whole adventure : that, as he was seeking a camel he had lost, he found himself on a sudden at the gates of this city, and entering it, saw not one inhabitant, at which being terrified, he stayed no longer than to take with him some fine stones which he showed the Khalif."—*Sale's Koran*.

Sudi says that Hafiz composed this poem in a beautiful garden belonging to Shah Shudja, and called by him the Bagh-i-Irem, after Shedad's legendary Paradise.

" Il y avait jadis en Perse un grand roi nommé Djem ou Djemshid. Il régna sept cents ans ; je ne saurai vous dire à quelle date au juste, mais ' tant qu'il régna, il n'y eut dans son empire ni mort, ni maladie, ni vieillesse, et tous les hommes marchaient dans la taille de jouvenceaux de quinze ans ; il n'y avait ni chaleur, ni froideur, et jamais ne se desséchaient les eaux ni les plantes.' Mais le pauvre Djem n'avait point la tête solide, et, comme il faisait des immortels, il se crut Dieu et voulut être adoré. Aussitôt, le Fari Yazdan, c'est-à-dire la gloire royale qui vient de Dieu, l'abandonna ; un serpent à trois têtes, nommé Zohab, vint de l'Arabie et lui prit son trône ; il s'enfuit dans l'Inde et y resta chaché mille ans durant ; puis un beau jour, s'étant aventuré hors de sa retraite, il fut livré au serpent, qui le scia en deux avec une arête de poisson. Entre autres splendeurs, le roi Djemshid, au temps de sa splendeur, possé-dait une coupe magique où il voyait tout l'univers et tout ce qui s'y passe. Certains savants prétendent que cette coupe était le soleil qui voit toute chose ; d'autres, que c'était un globe terrestre mis au courant, et il me souvient qu'il y a deux ans, prenant le thé dans un café de Stamboul avec un sage d'Isfahan, nommé Habib, la conversation tomba de la tasse de thé à la coupe de Djemshid, et Habib, me mettant le doigt au front, me dit : Djam-i-Djemshid, dil-i-agah : " la coupe de Djemshid c'est le cœur de l'homme de science."—*Darmsteter, " Lettres sur l'Inde.*"

A few miles from Peshawar, Darmsteter goes on to relate, there is a dried-up pond called the Talab i Djemshid, into which the King is said to have cast his magic cup. The head man of the village told the French traveller that a knife had been discovered there bearing this inscription : " This pond was dug by me, Djemshid, five hundred years before the Hejra." " Elle n'a pas été retrouvée, la coupe de Djemshid," adds Darmsteter, " non plus que la coupe du roi de Thulé, c'est pour ça qu'il n'y a plus parmi les hommes ni science, ni amour."

Djemshid is supposed to have built Persepolis. There is a legend that his cup was found buried in its foundations, and that it was formed of an enormous turquoise. It is said that he was the first to drink wine, and that he recommended it to his subjects as a health-giving beverage. He, too, was the father of chemistry and the possessor of the philospher's stone.

III

Stanza 1.—King Solomon sent the lapwing or hoopoe as his messenger to Bilkis, Queen of Sheba. The story is told thus by Al Ta'labi, in his Stories of the Prophets. (The lapwing had already made a journey on his own account, and had brought Solomon news of the great Queen, and told him that she was not a worshipper of the true God.) "Then Solomon wrote a letter saying : From the servant of God, Solomon, son of David, to Bilkis, Queen of Saba, in the name of God the Merciful, the Compassionate, peace be upon him who follows the right road. After which he said : Behave not insolently towards me, but come unto me humbled. And he strewed musk upon it and sealed it with his seal. Then he said to the lapwing : Fly with this letter and deliver it unto them, then turn away, but remain near them and hear what answer they make. And the lapwing took the letter and flew with it to Bilkis. And she was in the land which is called Marib, at a distance of three days' journey, and she had entered into her castle, and the gates of it were shut. For when she slept she was wont to shut the gates and to take the key and lay it beneath her head. So the lapwing came unto her, and she was asleep, lying upon her back ; and he laid the letter upon her breast. Wahb ibn Manabbih says that there was a window opposite to the sun so that the sunbeams fell through it at dawn, and when she saw the sun she was wont to bow down and worship it. And the lapwing went to this window and blocked it up with his wings. And the sun rose, but she knew it not. And she thought that the sun was late, and stood up to look for it. Then the lapwing threw a leaf upon her face. And they say that Bilkis took the letter and she was able to read the writing. But when she saw the seal she trembled and bowed down, because of the power of Solomon that was in his seal. For she knew that the power of him who had sent the letter was greater than hers, and she said : Lo, here is a king whose messengers are the birds ; verily he is a mighty king."

Stanzas 5 and 6.—The accepted explanation of these lines is that by the glass Hafiz means his own heart, which he sends to his mistress that she may see that her own image is reflected in it ; but I prefer here (and indeed for the whole poem) a mystical interpretation. The heavenly voice tells him to seek for comfort in Sufiism, and bids him look upon the mirror, for he shall see God himself reflected in it—which is only another way of putting the doctrine that man and God are one. The poet's reputation has gained him admittance into the company of the Sufis, let him hasten to them, for they shall give him that for which he seeks.

A horse and robe is the Eastern gift of honour. Lane in one of his notes to the "Arabian Nights" quotes a significant story concerning these gifts: "A person chancing to look at a register kept by one of the officers of Harun al Rashid, saw in it the following entry: '400,000 pieces of gold, the price of a dress of honour for Jafar ibn Yahya, the Vizir.' A few days after he saw beneath this written: 'Ten kerits, the price of naphtha and reeds for burning the body of Jafar ibn Yahya.' (The kerit of Baghdad was worth a twentieth part of a gold piece.)

Put not your trust in Eastern princes!

IV

Verse 3.—The Persians describe the dimple in the chin of their mistress as a dangerous well filled with her lover's tears, into which, when he approaches her mouth, he may fall and be drowned.

Verse 6.—"Oh rose, tearing thy robe in two": that is, bursting into flower beneath the warm breath of the wind that blows from where thou art.

V

Stanza 1.—When the conqueror Timur entered Shiraz it is related that he summoned Hafiz before him and said: "Of all my empire, Bokhara and Samarkand are the fairest jewels; how comes it that in thy song thou hast declared that thou would'st exchange them against the black mole on the cheek of thy mistress?" Hafiz replied: "It is because of such generosity that I am now as poor as thou seest." The Emperor was not to be outdone in repartee: he sent the poet away a richer man by some hundreds of gold pieces.

NOTES

" C'est du Molière renversé," says Darmsteter of these lines, and quotes :—

" Si le roi m'avait donné
Paris sa grande ville,
Et qu'il me fallût quitter
L'amour de ma mie,
Je dirais au roi Henri :
Reprenez votre Paris,
J'aime mieux ma mie, ô gué,
J'aime mieux ma mie ! "

In the garden of Mosalla, Hafiz lies buried ; the stream Ruknabad flows near at hand.

Stanza 2.—The Luli or gipsies, as they were contemptuously called, were a people of the tribe of Keredj, of Indian origin, who inhabited the country between Shiraz and Isfahan. Their young men and maidens were famous for their beauty and musical accomplishments, and furnished minstrels and dancing girls to the wealthy inhabitants of Shiraz. Sir Henry Layard met with a similar tribe near Baghdad. " They bear," he says, " a very bad reputation on the score of morality, and according to general report lead very dissolute lives. The dancing boys and girls who frequent Baghdad, and are notoriously of evil fame, come principally from this district. Whilst we were resting at the caravanserai a party of them came to perform their indecent dances before us, as they were in the habit of doing on the arrival of travellers."—*Early Adventures*.

In Turkestan there was formerly an institution called the Feast of Plunder. When the pay-day of the soldiers came round, dishes of rice and great quantities of cooked food were prepared and set out on the ground. The soldiers then rode up, armed as if for battle, and carried off the food with mimic violence. Thus they made reparation to their conscience for accepting a pay lawfully earned, and reminded themselves that rapine was their true profession.

Stanza 3.—Joseph is the Oriental type of perfect beauty. The story of his relations with Zuleikha, Potiphar's wife, is one of the famous love stories of the East ; Jami made it the theme of a long metaphysical poem. The part played by Zuleikha in Persian tales is far more creditable than that which is assigned to her either in the Bible or the Koran.

Every translator of Hafiz has tried his hand upon this song, which is one of the most famous in the Divan. It is only right to inform the reader that the original is of great beauty.

The whole poem has received a mystical interpretation which seems to me to add but little to its value or to its intelligibility ; but in case any one should wish to gather the higher wisdom from it, I may mention that the mole, powder, and paint, of which a beautiful face does not stand in need, represent the ink, colour, dots, and lines of the Koran ; and this is the explanation given to the couplet concerning Joseph and Zuleikha by a thorough-going Western mystic : " By reason of that beauty daily increasing that Joseph (the absolute existence, the real beloved, God) had, I (the first day) knew that love for him would bring Zuleikha (us, things possible) forth from the screen of chastity (the pure existence of God)." The learned translator seems to have felt that his version presented some difficulties, and he adds for the use of his weaker brethren the following comment : " In the world of non-existence and possibility, when I beheld the splendour of true beauty with different qualities, I knew for certain that Love would take us out of the ambush." This makes everything clear.

VII

Stanza 1.—Those who have seen a Persian garden will not find it difficult to understand why it should play so large a part in Persian poetry. Often enough you may pass with one step out of a barren desert of dust and stones into one of these green and fertile spots, full of violets in the spring, and of roses and lilies in the early summer ; and from the blinding glare of a Persian sun into a cool and shadowy retreat planted with great plane-trees. The water which flows in numberless streams through the garden, and leaps in countless fountains, has worked all the miracle. The change from desert to flowery paradise is one of those strong contrasts so common in the East which take hold of the imagination of all who see them.

Stanza 3.—That is, do not attempt to light the torches of a Mahommadan monastery from the lamp of a Jewish synagogue. One of the most famous of the Prophet's sayings is : there is no monasticism in Islam. Nevertheless, from the time of Abu Bekr and Ali onwards, such religious associations grew up and flourished. Nearly all the celebrated doctors of whom the Sufis boast in the first six hundred years after the Hejra belonged to them.

" Verily our messengers write down that which ye deceitfully devise," says the Koran (chap. x.). Two guardian angels attend every man and write down his actions ; they are changed daily and a fresh pair takes their place. The books which they have written shall be produced on the Day of Judgment.

Stanza 4.—It was this verse which decided the right of Hafiz to receive honourable burial.

VIII

Stanza 3.—When God had created man and made him wiser than the angels, he bound him to himself by a solemn treaty. " Am I not thy Lord who has created thee ? " he demanded, and man answered " Yes." But the Arabic word *bala*, which signifies assent, means also sorrow, and they say that the first of our fathers knew full well what a terrible gift was that life which he had received from his Lord, and sealed the treaty with a seal of grief. Therefore since the earliest day, life and sorrow have gone hand in hand, bound together by the first great pact between God and man.

NOTES

Stanza 4.—Compare François Villon's rough and powerful treatment of the same theme :—

> " Où sont de Vienne et de Grenobles
> Le Dauphin, les preux, les senés ?
> Où de Dijon, Sallin et Dolles,
> Les sires et les fils aînés ?
> Où autant de leurs gens privés,
> Hérauts, trompettes, poursuivants ?
> Ont-ils bien bouté sous le nez ? . . .
> Autant en emporte le vent ! "

Solomon, the type of human greatness, is the King whose mastery has left nothing behind. He harnessed the wind as a steed to his chariot, he spoke with the birds in their own tongue, and the wise and magnificent Assaf was his minister. Upon his seal was engraved the name of God which is unknown to men and before which the Jinn and the Angels must bow down. It was with this seal that he fastened up the bottles in which he imprisoned the Jinn—those bottles which the fishermen in the " Arabian Nights " pull up in their nets.

IX

Stanza 1.—This poem is addressed to the Vizir of Sultan Oweis of Baghdad, Hadji Kawameddin, who founded a college for Hafiz in Shiraz. With true Persian exaggeration the poet must needs write to his patron much in the same terms in which a lover would write to his mistress ; but his words, though they sound strangely to our ears, are nothing more than the Oriental way of saying, " Awake, my St. John ! "

The mystical interpretation of the first few lines is said to be : As the wine glows in the cup like the reflection of a ruddy cheek, so in the goblet of my heart I have seen the reflection of God, the true Beloved.

Stanza 6.—It is related that upon a certain occasion when Hafiz was feasting with the Vizir in the latter's garden, a servant handed to him a goblet of wine, and as he took it he saw in it the reflection of the crescent moon overhead. The incident suggested this verse to him. I should say that the anecdote was of doubtful authenticity.

X

This song is not to be found in the best editions of the Divan, and is believed to be spurious; but it is printed in most of the popular editions, and is as widely known as any of the poems which pass with a better right under the name of Hafiz. It is set to a soft and well-nigh tuneless air which sounds like dream music, or the echo of something very beautiful coming from a great distance, the singer ending on an almost whispered repetition of the first exquisite phrase. I have been told that the boatmen on the Ganges sing it as they row, and the monotonous accompaniment of the water under the oars must be even more fitting to the melody than that of the lute strings.

XI

Stanza 2.—I have found no explanation of these difficult lines, and, for want of a better, I venture to suggest the following: the Garden of Irem, as has been said in the Note to Poem II., was a mimic Paradise constructed by a certain fabulous King Shedad, who wished to be considered a rival to his Maker by his fellows, for which temerity a swift and sharp judgment fell upon him; the River of Life is one of the many streams which waters the divine Paradise. To my thinking, Hafiz takes the one as a type of the wildest human ambition, the other as a part of the most beautiful vision which the mind of man has conceived. And to what does it all amount? he asks. Only to this: that we are like to one who sits and dreams upon the banks of a mighty and resistless river, fed from many sources, and sings, if he be wise, his song of praise, and so departs.

Stanza 4.—The river Kausar is another of the streams of Paradise; indeed, it is said to be the central spring from whence all the others flow. A part of its waters are led into a great square lake, a month's journey in compass. On the banks of this lake the souls of good Mahommadans rest and find refreshment after they have crossed the terrible bridge, sharper than the edge of a sword, which is laid over the midst of Hell. The waters of the lake are whiter than silver and sweeter than musk. Round it are set as many cups as there are stars in the firmament, and he who has drunk of it shall thirst no more.

XIV

Stanza 1.—Hafiz wrote this poem upon the death of his son.

Stanza 3.—Rosenzweig, in his edition of the Divan, says that the allusion is to the dust and water which God kneaded into the body of Adam, and that, out of derision, Hafiz calls the human body a house of joy.

The moon, according to Persian superstition, has a baneful influence upon human life.

Stanza 4.—Rosenzweig says that " I had not castled " means that Hafiz had not taken the precaution of marrying his son, and so securing for himself grandchildren who would have been a consolation to him on their father's death. For that reason he had nothing more to lose, and was indifferent as to what his next move in the game should be.

XV

Stanza 3.—" Night is with child "—a Persian proverb extraordinarily suggestive of the clear, deep, Eastern sky. The sight seems to slip through between the stars and penetrate a darkness which is big with possibilities.

NOTES

XVI

Stanza 2.—These lines are exceedingly mysterious, as, indeed, is the whole poem. I have looked for an explanation of them in other editions of Hafiz, but have found little more than a bare translation of the Persian words. For the meaning of this stanza, see Introduction, p. 74.

Sidreh and Tuba are two trees in the Garden of Paradise. The former is the abode of the angel Gabriel. Concerning the latter Sale says : " They fable that it stands in the palace of Mahommad, though a branch of it will reach to the house of every true believer ; that it will be laden with pomegranates, grapes, dates, and other fruits of surprising bigness, and of tastes unknown to mortals. So that if a man desire to eat of any particular kind of fruit, it will immediately be presented to him ; or if he choose flesh, birds ready dressed will be set before him, according to his wish. They add that the boughs of this tree will spontaneously bend down to the hand of the person who would gather of its fruits, and that it will supply the blessed not only with food, but also with silken garments and beasts to ride on, ready saddled and bridled and adorned with rich trappings, which will burst forth from its fruits ; and that this tree is so large that a person mounted on the fleetest horse would not be able to gallop from one end of its shade to the other in a hundred years."—*Introduction to the Koran.*

Stanza 4.—He means either *facilis descensus Averni*, or, more probably, that a great number of those upon whom the orthodox look askance will be found to have equal claim to reward, since the distinction between Sufi and orthodox is in fact nothing.

Stanza 5.—" The lovers of wine "—that is to say the Sufis, who will be equally indifferent whether he comes to them with or without trailing clouds of human approbation, since they will judge of his worth by a different standard.

NOTES

XVII

Stanza 3.—The allusion is to the expulsion of Adam from the Garden of Eden.

Stanza 4.—Concerning the Last Judgment, a beautiful tradition relates that there are seven degrees of punishment, but eight of blessedness, because God's mercy exceeds His justice.

XVIII

Stanza 1.—Blue is the Persian colour of mourning. Hafiz compares the weeping lovers, clad in robes of grief, to a bed of violets, and as the violets bow their heads when the wind passes over them, so they bow down when their mistress passes by with flowing curls.

Stanza 3.—" Erghwan," the Syringa Persica or Persian lilac. In the early spring, before it comes into leaf, it is covered with buds of a beautiful reddish-purple colour.

" Khizr," a prophet whom the Mahommadans confound with Phineas, Elias, and St. George, saying that his soul passed by metempsychosis successively through all three. He discovered the fountain of life and drank of it, thereby making himself immortal. It is said that he guided Alexander to the same fountain, which lay in the Land of Darkness. It was he, too, for whom Moses set out to seek when he had been informed by God that Al Khizr was wiser than he. He found him seated on a rock, at the meeting of the two seas, and followed him for a time, learning wisdom from him, as is related in the eighteenth chapter of the Koran. His name signifies Green ; wherever his feet rested, the earth was covered with green herbs.

Hafiz looked upon the prophet Al Khizr as one of his special guardians. About four Persian miles from Shiraz there is a spot called Pir-i-Sabz, the Old Green Man ; whosoever should pass forty nights in it without sleeping, on the fortieth night

Al Khizr would appear to him and confer upon him the immortal gift of song. Hafiz in his youth fell in love with a beautiful girl of Shiraz called Shakh-i-Nahat, and in order to win her heart he determined to meet Al Khizr and receive from him the art of poetry. For thirty-nine mornings he walked beneath the windows of Shakh-i-Nahat, at noon he ate, then he slept, and at night he kept watch, undismayed by the terrible apparition of a fierce lion which was his nightly companion. At length, on the fortieth morning, Shakh-i-Nahat called him into her house and told him that she was ready to become his wife, for she preferred a man of genius to the son of a king. She would have kept him with her, but Hafiz, though he had gained his original end, was now filled with desire to become a poet, and insisted upon keeping his fortieth vigil. That night an old man dressed in green garments came to him and brought him a cup of the water of immortality.

XIX

Stanza 2.—See Note to Stanza 1 of Poem III.

Stanza 5.—" Narrow-eyedness " is the exact translation of the Persian word for greed, and there is consequently, in the original, a play of meaning between the physical and moral attributes of the Tartars.

It is significant that Hafiz should choose the " narrow-eyed " Tartar robbers as types of cruelty. Just as the Anglo-Saxons prayed to be delivered from the Danes, so a clause in the Persian litany of the thirteenth and fourteenth centuries might have been : " From the power of the Tartars, good Lord, deliver us ! " First under Hulagu, and then under Timur, they overran and devastated Persia. The destruction wrought by them was very similar to that wrought by the Arab conquerors in the Roman provinces of North Africa. They rased to the ground great cities ; they reduced populous and fertile regions to a barren desert by breaking down the old reservoirs and destroying the irrigating system, completely changing the physical conditions of parts of the country. In the mountains to the north of Tehran, for instance, there are villages bearing names the etymology of which points to their having stood at the outlet of a reservoir of which no other trace remains, and it is said that the country surrounding the town was far more thoroughly irrigated before the Tartar invasion, and supported a larger population. The invaders completely destroyed the ancient city of Rhages, which lay at a distance of about three miles from the modern capital. The same thing happened in North Africa. The ruins of Roman towns are to be found in country which must once have been fertile, but which is now reconquered by the sands of the Sahara.

" One poor robe." The Persian runs : " man dervish-i-yek kaba "—*i.e.* I, a poor man of one robe—*dervish* signifying in its primary sense, it is hardly necessary to say, *poor*. I should think that the double meaning is significant. In its mystical sense, the poem describes how Hafiz found consolation in the ecstatic drunkenness of the Sufis, in the minstrel's song, or divine message, which brought him a word from God ; and when finally the last shred of his orthodoxy had been torn from him, when in his desperate struggle with existence he was forced to abandon even his dervish robe, Heaven mercifully showed him a safe refuge in the Sufi doctrines.

XXI

Stanza 1.—Sir Henry Layard gives the following account of a party of dervishes with whom he travelled, from which it would appear that the contempt of Hafiz for the dervish habit was not wholly uncalled for : " They were a picturesque and motley crew. One or two of them were what the Persians call *luti*, young men with well-dyed curls, long garments, and conical caps embroidered in many colours—debauched and dissolute fellows, who, under the guise of poverty, and affecting abstinence and piety, were given to every manner of vice.

Others were half-naked savages, with hair hanging down their backs, and the skins of gazelles on their shoulders—bare-footed, dirty, and covered with vermin. They carried heavy iron maces, and seemed more disposed to exact than to ask for charity. As they went along they shouted 'Yah Allah! yah Muhammad! yah Ali!' They all had slung from their shoulders the carved cocoa-nut shell, which is indispensable to the dervish, and serves for carrying food and for drinking purposes. Round their necks they wore charms and amulets, with beads and coloured strings and tassels." He goes on to say: "Most Persian dervishes, although they have great pretensions to sanctity, by which they impose upon the people, high and low, are without any religion. They are, however, credited with working miracles, and with being able to give efficacious charms. . . . Although these dervishes are rank impostors, and generally arrant scoundrels, they maintain their influence over the ignorant and superstitious Persians of all classes, who greatly fear, and do not dare to offend them. Consequently no one ventures to refuse them admission into their houses, and even into the women's apartments, where those who go stark-naked, and are looked upon as specially holy and protected by Allah and Ali, can enter with impunity. Sometimes they will demand a specific sum of money from a rich man, and if he refuses to pay it, will establish themselves in the gateway or porch of his dwelling, or outside close to it, and enclosing a small plot of ground, sow wheat or plant flowers, and remain until what they ask for is paid them, hooting hideously day and night, calling upon Mohammad, Ali, and the Imams, or blowing on a buffalo's horn so as to disturb the whole neighbourhood. The owner and inmates of the house are helpless. They do not dare to remove by force the holy men."—*Early Adventures*.

Stanza 2.—That is to say, the prayer-carpet of the orthodox Mussulman had not enough value to procure for him so much as one glass of Sufi wine. Nor was he worthy to lay his head even upon the dusty steps of the tavern—the place of instruction in Sufi doctrine.

NOTES

Stanza 3.—To be clothed in one colour is the Persian idiom for sincerity. He means that the single purple robe of the grape is worth more than the hypocritical garment of the dervish, all torn and patched with long journeying—in the wrong road.

Stanza 5.—So far I have endeavoured to give the mystical interpretation of the poem. There is, however, a story attached to it which turns it into a historical rather than a theological document. It is related that the King of the Deccan, Mahmud Shah Bahmani, had heard of the fame of Hafiz, and having a pretty taste in literature, was desirous of attracting him to his court. Accordingly he ordered his Vizir, Mir Feiz Allah Inju, to send the poet a sufficient sum to pay for his journey from Shiraz. Hafiz resolved to accept the invitation. He wound up his affairs in his native town, using some of the money the Sultan had sent him in paying his debts and in making gifts to his sister's children, and set forth upon his journey. But when he reached the town of Lar he found there an acquaintance in very bad case, having been plundered by robbers and reduced to a state of beggary. Hafiz was moved to compassion and gave him the remainder of the money which Mahmud Shah had sent to him. He was now himself unable to continue his journey for want of means, and perhaps it was bitter experience that taught him that in very fact his prayer-carpet would not fetch him a glass of wine, and that without the necessary silver pieces he would be thrust from out the tavern doors. From these straits he was rescued by two friendly merchants, who were also on their way to India, and who offered to pay his expenses to Hormuz, and there place him on a vessel of Mahmud Shah's which was coming to fetch them. Hafiz accepted the offer, went to Hormuz, and embarked on the ship. But before they had left the port a violent storm arose, and persuaded the poet that no advantages he might reap from the journey would be worth the sorrow of the sea. Under pretext of bidding farewell to some friends, he disembarked, and in all haste made the best of his way back to Shiraz, sending to Feiz Allah this poem as an excuse for failing to keep his engagement. The Vizir read it to Mahmud Shah, who was transported by the beauty of the verses and the philosophic dignity in which Hafiz had cloaked his fears of the dangers of the road and the discomforts of sea-sickness. With singular generosity he sent the defaulting poet a further present, consisting of some at least of the riches of his lands and seas.

XXIII

This poem is said to have been written by Hafiz upon the death of his wife.

XXIV

Stanza 5.—Shah Shudja, as has been related in the Introduction, was not always on the best of terms with Hafiz, partly because he was jealous of the latter's fame as a poet, and partly because Hafiz had been the protégé of Shah Shudja's former rival, Abu Ishac. Accordingly the King looked about for some means of doing the poet an injury, nor was it long before he found what he sought. He accused Hafiz of denying the Resurrection, basing the accusation upon the last couplet of this poem—the last three lines of the present translation—and cited him before the Ulema as an infidel. But Hafiz was too many for him. Before the day on which he was to answer the charge against himself, he inserted another couplet into the ode, in which he stated that the dangerous lines did not express his own opinion, but that of a heretical Christian. He came off with flying colours; for not only was he entirely cleared, but it was also acknowledged that he had dealt a good blow on behalf of the Mahommadan religion, since he had shown up one of the errors of the infidel.

XXV

Stanza 1.—There are many ways of taking omens which are still practised by the Persians. Concerning astrology and geomancy Mr. Browne questioned a learned Persian, and received the reply that there was positive proof of their truth. The Persian added, however, that the study of these sciences was very difficult, and many who professed to be acquainted with them were mere charlatans. Many dreams also, he said, were capable of interpretation, and might furnish indications to events which were yet to come. Mr. Browne relates that he consulted a geomancer, who, by means of dice, gave him much information as to his future—none of which has yet been justified by the event—but on being asked to perform the less difficult task of answering some questions as to his past, turned the conversation into other channels. "I discussed," says the traveller, "the occult sciences with several of my friends, to discover as far as possible the prevailing opinion among them. One of them made use of the following argument to prove their existence: "God," he said, "has no *bukhl* (avarice); it is impossible for Him to withhold from any one a thing for which he strives with sufficient earnestness. Just as if a man devotes all his energies to the pursuit of spiritual knowledge he attains to it, so if he chooses to make occult sciences and magical powers the object of his aspirations they will assuredly not be withheld from him."—*A Year Amongst the Persians.*

An omen can be taken by opening the Koran or some other well-accredited book (the Divan of Hafiz among the number), pricking a pin into the page, and following whatever directions can be drawn from the verse thus indicated. This method is frequently used before setting out upon a journey. The stars also are consulted in order to select a favourable day for embarking upon any enterprise, certain stars having special influence over men—the influence of the moon, for instance, is dangerous to life, and one of the stars in the constellation of Cassiopea is of evil presage. Besides these omens, divinations are taken from the movements and position of certain animals and birds, and from various passing events. To meet a one-eyed man is of bad omen, especially if he is blind of the left eye, or to hear an unlucky word on setting out from your house of a morning. Lane, in one of his notes to the "Arabian

Nights," tells of a Sultan who was setting out on a raid, when one of his standards happening to strike against a cluster (or Pleiades, as they are called in Arabic) of lamps, he regarded this to be of evil import, and was about to abandon the expedition. " Oh our lord ! " said one of his officers, " our standards have reached the Pleiades." The Sultan, encouraged by this fortunate suggestion, continued on his way, and returned victorious.

XXVI

Stanza 2.—For Djemshid, see Note to Stanza 2 of Poem II. He was the fourth king of the First or Pishdadian dynasty, and is supposed to have flourished eight hundred years before the Christian era. Firdusi says he reigned seven hundred years. Kaikobad was the founder of the Second dynasty, the Kayanian. He was set upon the throne by the hero Rustum, son of Zal. It was in his reign that Rustum overcame Afrasiab's army, killing his own son in the battle " by the great Oxus stream, the yellow Oxus," a story which all readers of Matthew Arnold know. Kaikobad is said to have reigned one hundred and twenty years. Bahman, another member of the Kayanian house, is better known to the Persians as Ardisher Dirazdast, the Artaxerxes Longimanus of the Greeks. He came to the throne in B.C. 464. He was the grandson of Darius, the Persian Gushtasp. He is supposed to have been the Ahasuerus of Scripture who married Esther. Persian historians ascribe to him also remarkable longevity, and state that he reigned one hundred and twelve years. Kaikaus, mentioned in the next stanza, was the son of Kaikobad, second king of the Kayanian dynasty ; Kai may be Kaikhusro, the third king of the same dynasty.

Stanza 3.—The loves of Ferhad and Shirin are famous in Persian legend. Shirin is called by some Mary, and by others Irene. The Greeks describe her as a Roman by birth and a Christian ; the Turks and the Persians say that she was a daughter of the Emperor Maurice, and wife of Khusro Parwiz, who came to the Persian throne in A.D. 591. It was Khusro Parwiz who conquered Jerusalem, and carried off, say the Persians, the true Cross, which had been enclosed in a gold box and buried in the ground. He was devotedly attached to his wife Shirin, but she had given her heart to her humble lover Ferhad. He, despairing of ever reaching one whose rank had placed her so far above him, wandered through the deserts and the mountains of Persia calling upon her name, and in order to beguile his weary hours executed the sculptures upon the rock Behistun—so says the legend. At length the King sent to him and told him that if he would cut through the rock and cause a stream upon the other side of the mountains to flow through it, he would relinquish Shirin to him. Ferhad set himself to the task, and had almost accomplished it when Khusro sent him the false news of Shirin's death. On hearing it, Ferhad threw himself from the top of the rock and so died. Shirin's end was scarcely less tragic. Khusro Parwiz was put to a violent death by his son, who proceeded to make proposals of marriage to his father's widow. Shirin promised to marry him if he would allow her to see once more her husband's corpse. She was led to the place where the murdered King lay, and drawing a dagger, she stabbed herself and fell dead across his body.

It is difficult to conceive anything more exquisite than the little scarlet tulip growing upon a barren Persian hillside. On the top of a bleak pass over the mountains between Resht and Tehran, I have seen companies of tiny tulips shining like jewels among the dust and stones.

There is a tradition that this poem was sent to the King of Golconda.

XXVIII

Stanza I.—According to Oriental belief, Jesus Christ's gift of healing was due to a miraculous quality in His breath.

NOTES

XXIX

Stanza 3.—Maghilan, a thorny shrub which grows on the deserts of Arabia near to Mecca. When the pilgrims see it they know that they have almost reached their goal, and forget the hardships of the journey and the barrenness of the wastes through which their road lies.

XXX

Stanza 1.—Khizr—see Note to the third stanza of Poem XVIII.

Stanza 2.—The quarter of Jafrabad has ceased to exist. Its position was to the east of the town, opposite to the fields and to the ruined mosque of Mosalla. Between Jafrabad and Mosalla runs the highroad to Isfahan, traversing, at the distance of a mile from Shiraz, the pass of Allahu Akbar.

The angel Gabriel, the Holy Spirit, is the highest of all the angels. It is his duty to write down the decrees of God; through him the Koran was revealed to Mahommad, and it is he who, hovering above the throne of God, shelters it with his wings. Hafiz therefore claims for Shiraz the protection of him who is guardian of the highest place in heaven.

Ibn Batuta, the Arab traveller who visited Shiraz about the year 1340, has left a charming description of the native town of Hafiz and of the manners of his contemporaries. "Shiraz," he says, "is a well-built town of a great size, a wide celebrity, and a high place among cities. It possesses pleasant gardens, far-reaching streams, excellent markets, fine streets, and a numerous population. The town is constructed with taste and admirably arranged; each trade has its own bazaar. The inhabitants are a fine race and well clad. Shiraz lies in a plain; gardens surround it on every side; and five rivers flow through it, amongst them one called Ruknabad, a stream of which the water is excellent to drink, very cold in summer and warm in winter. The principal mosque is called the Old Mosque; it is as spacious and as well built as any one could wish to see. The court of it is vast and paved with marble ; in hot weather it is washed with fresh water every night. The wealthy citizens come there every evening to repeat the prayers of sunset and of night. The inhabitants of Shiraz are well-to-do, pious, and chaste ; the women in particular are distinguished for their modesty. They go completely veiled, give much in alms, and repair three times a week to the great mosque. Often as many as two thousand are assembled there, sitting with fans in their hands on account of the great heat. Each day in one of the mausoleums the whole Koran is read aloud, and the readers have very beautiful voices. The people bring with them fruits and sweetmeats, and when the congregation has finished eating, the preacher begins his discourse. This takes place between the mid-day and the evening prayers." Ibn Batuta struck up acquaintance with a Sheikh whom he found seated in a small hermitage at the corner of a mosque. The Sheikh was engaged in reading the Koran. In answer to Ibn Batuta's questions, he told him that he had founded the mosque himself, and that the hermitage was to be his tomb. Lifting a carpet, he showed him his grave, covered over with planks. " In that box," he said, pointing to a chest opposite to him, " are my winding-sheet, some spices with which my corpse will be perfumed, and a few pieces of money which I earned by digging a well for a pious man. The money will serve to pay for my burial, and what is left over will be distributed among the poor." " I admired his conduct," adds Ibn Batuta. " One of the mausoleums outside the town," he continues, " contains the tomb of Sheikh Sa'di, the first poet of his time. Close at hand is a hermitage built by Sa'di himself, surrounded by a charming garden. It is situated near the source of the Ruknabad. In the garden Sheikh Sa'di constructed a number of basins for the washing of clothes. The citizens of Shiraz make parties of pleasure to this mausoleum ; they eat food prepared in the hermitage, wash their garments in the river, and at sunset return to the town. So did I also. May God have mercy on Shiraz ! " he concludes piously.

NOTES

XXXI

Stanza 3.—The month of Sha'aban is the eighth month of the Arabic year. It is followed by Ramazan, during which month the Prophet decreed that from two hours before dawn until sunset nothing should pass the lips of his followers. The fast is so strictly observed, especially by the lower orders, that not only do they refrain from eating and drinking, but they will not even smoke until the sunset gun puts an end to the day's abstinence. The night, however, is passed in feasting and revelry, and the richer classes will sleep late in Ramazan and shorten the long hours that must pass before they may breakfast.

XXXII

Stanza 3.—According to the popular science of the East, the colouring of precious stones, even of those which are buried deep in the earth, is due to the action of rain and wind and of the rays of the sun.

Stanza 4.—It is a favourite Persian image to describe the hair of the beloved as entangling and entrapping the unfortunate lover. Her long locks are often compared to deadly snakes, and her curls to hooks which catch and tear her lover's heart. One need go no further than the *Merchant of Venice* to find the same imagery used by a Western poet : " Those crisped snaky golden locks," and again, " A golden mesh to entrap the hearts of men faster than gnats in cobwebs."

XXXIV

Stanza 1.—The story of the creation of Adam, and of the part played in it by the angels, is told by Mahommad in the following terms : " When thy Lord said unto the angels, I am going to place a substitute on earth ; they said, Wilt thou place there one who will do evil therein, and shed blood ? but we celebrate thy praise and sanctify thee. God answered, Verily I know that which ye know not ; and he taught Adam the names of all things, and then proposed them to the angels, and said, Declare unto me the names of these things if ye say truth. They answered, Praise be unto thee, we have no knowledge but what thou teachest us, for thou art knowing and wise. God said, Oh Adam, tell them their names. And when he had told them their names, God said, Did I not tell you that I know the secrets of heaven and earth, and know that which ye discover and that which ye conceal ? And when we said unto the angels, Worship Adam ; they all worshipped him, except Eblis, who refused, and was puffed up with pride, and became of the number of unbelievers."—*Koran,* chap. ii.

Tradition has amplified and adorned this story. It is said that the three archangels, Gabriel, Michael, and Israfil, were each in turn ordered to take from the earth seven handfuls of clay of three different colours, red, white, and yellow, that God might create out of it the races of mankind. But each in turn was moved by the earth's prayer that he would not rob her of her substance, and each returned to heaven empty-handed. The fourth time God sent Azrail, the angel of death, who tore the seven handfuls from the earth, but hearing her lamentations, promised her that when man ceased to live his substance should return to the earth from whence it had been taken. With the clay that Azrail brought him God moulded the figure of man, and when it was finished he left it forty days to dry. The angels came often to gaze upon it, and Eblis, kicking it with his foot, found that it rang hollow. When the figure of clay was dry, God breathed the breath of life into its nostrils, and ordered the angels to submit to the man he had created. But Eblis refused, saying that he had been created of pure fire, and would not serve a hollow mould of clay ; for which reason God cast him out of Paradise. The rest of the angels acknowledged the superiority of Adam after God had made him tell them the names of all the creatures of the earth, though they had at first protested that it was not seemly that they should bow down to him, for their love for God was greater than his. It is with this legend in his mind that Hafiz speaks of the angels as standing at the tavern door, where man may enter and receive instruction in God's wisdom, but where they must knock in vain, and as moulding a wine-cup with the despised clay out of which the human body was moulded. I think he means that man himself is the vessel into which divine love and wisdom are poured; and when he says that the angels first brought him wine, he means that by their example they showed him what it was to be intoxicated by the contemplation of God.

Stanza 3.—"Concerning the forbidden fruit," says Sale in a note to the second chapter of the Koran, "the Mohammadans, as well as the Christians, have different opinions. Some say it was an ear of wheat, some will have it to have been a fig-tree, and others a vine."

There are supposed to be seventy-two sects in Islam. Many Mahommadan writers compare them to the seventy-two branches of the family of Noah after the Babylonian confusion of tongues and the dispersal of the children of Adam.

XXXV

Stanza 1.—The second line of this poem is as often quoted as any, perhaps, in the Divan: "Yàd bàd àn ruz-i-gàràn, yàd bàd!" A man will set it upon a letter to an absent friend, even when he is not particularly anxious that days gone by should be preserved from oblivion; and how often must the simple little line have been used by those to whom its very simplicity made it more poignant than pages of sentiment!

Stanza 3.—The Zindeh Rud was a river that flowed past Isfahan. There are unfortunately no longer rose-gardens upon its banks, for it disappeared completely in the terrible earthquake which occurred in the spring of the year 1853. I suspect from internal evidence that this poem was sent to some friends of Hafiz living at Isfahan, upon whom the passionate appeal need reflect no discredit, since it may quite possibly be merely the Oriental way of writing a letter of thanks. At the same time, in spite of this rational explanation, it must be acknowledged that the meaning of the name Zindeh Rud is River of Life. I tremble to think into what a slough of mysticism the innocent little stream might be induced to guide us!

XXXVI

Stanza 2.—"Love and Faith," says Rosenzweig, is the name of a well-known Persian story which has been retold by many writers.

XXXVII

Stanza 4.—See Note to Stanza 4 of Poem XXXIII.

The word bezoar comes from two Arabic roots which signify the annihilator of poison. Murray gives several examples of its use by seventeenth and eighteenth century writers in the sense of an antidote, chiefly to snake bites. Topsell, for instance, in his book on Serpents (1607), remarks that "the juice of apples being drunk, and endive, are the proper Bezoar against the venom of a Phalangie"—whatever that may be. The word was also applied to various substances held as antidotes, especially to a concretion found in the stomach of some animals, formed of concentric layers of animal matter deposited round some foreign substance. This concretion was called the bezoar stone. The original sort was the lapis bezoar orientale obtained from the wild goat of Persia, which was in later times called the bezoar goat; also from various antelopes, &c. The lapis bezoar occidentale, obtained from the llamas of Peru, was less valued. The chamois yielded German bezoar. "The stone," says Frampton, in his "Joyful News," "is called the Bezaar, being approved good against Venome"; and Hawkins, in his "Voyage to the South Seas," talks about "the becunia and other beasts which breed the beazer stone."

NOTES

XXXIX

Stanza 1.—It is related that Ghiyasuddin Purabi, who succeeded his father to the throne of Bengal in the year 1367, fell sick. During his illness he was nursed by three faithful handmaidens whose names were Cypress, Tulip, and Rose, and owing to their care he eventually recovered. The rest of the Sultan's ladies were jealous of the gratitude that the three maidens had earned from Ghiyasuddin, and nicknamed them contemptuously "the three bath women," because they had washed the King's body while he was ill. He therefore determined to do them honour by commemorating their devotion in a poem, and to this end he composed the first line of a couplet, and ordered the poets of his court to complete the ode. The line ran thus: "Sàki hadis-i-sarvo gul o làleh miravad"—Cup-bearer, a tale runs of a Cypress, a Rose, and a Tulip. But the poets were unable to perform the task to the King's satisfaction, and at length some one suggested that the line should be sent to Hafiz of Shiraz, the fame of whose great skill had reached Bengal. This was accordingly done, and Hafiz composed the ode here translated, with which the Sultan (whose taste seems to have turned towards the discursive in poetry) was much delighted. The three cups of wine are an allusion to the three maidens who washed the King's body; the parrots of India are the court poets of Ghiyasuddin, and the Persian sweetmeat is the ode that Hafiz sent to Bengal.

Stanza 4.—Samir. Al Samiri belonged, say the Mahommadans, to a certain tribe among the Jews called the Samaritans, whence his name. In this the Mahommadans strangely betray their ignorance of history, for the Samaritans were not formed into a people, nor did they bear that name, until many ages later. Some say that he was a proselyte, but a hypocritical one, and originally of Kerman or some other country. His real name was Musa ibn Dhafar. He was a magician and an alchemist. Pharaoh employed him as a rival to Moses when the latter worked miracles with his hand and his staff, but Al

Samiri was unable to show wonders as great as those performed by Moses. It was he and not Aaron, according to Mahommadan tradition, who cast the golden calf. The calf was made of the ornaments of gold and silver and other materials which the Israelites had borrowed from the Egyptians ; for Aaron, who commanded in his brother's absence, having ordered Al Samiri to collect those ornaments from the people, who carried on a wicked commerce with them, and to keep them together till the return of Moses, Al Samiri, understanding the founder's art, put them all together into a furnace, to melt them down into one mass, which came out in the form of a calf. The Israelites, accustomed to the Egyptian idolatry, paying a religious worship to this image, Al Samiri went further, and took some dust from the footsteps of the horse of the angel Gabriel, who marched at the head of the people, and threw it into the mouth of the calf, which immediately began to low, and became animated ; for such was the virtue of that dust. (Sale, Notes to second and twenty-second chapters of the Koran.) Al Simiri is mentioned by name in the twenty-second chapter of the Koran : " Al Samiri led them astray."

XL

Stanza 2.—According to Persian superstition, the smoke of burning rue has the power to avert the evil eye.

XLII

Stanza 1.—Khizr. See Note to Stanza 3 of Poem XVIII.

Stanza 3.—Zohra is the planet Venus, the musician of the heavens, and the protector of all musicians and singers upon the earth. Zohra played a part in very ancient mythology. The Mahommadans borrowed and adapted the Magian legends concerning her, and their account runs as follows : Once upon a time the angels fell to marvelling over the wickedness of man and the ease with which he was led astray, notwithstanding the warnings sent down to him through the prophets. But God, hearing their words, determined to expose them also to temptation, that they might learn how easy it was to fall. Therefore he appointed two of them, whose names were Harut and Marut, to go down to the earth as judges over man, and he taught them a secret word by the power of which every evening, when their work of judgment was done, they could return to heaven. For some time the two angels accomplished their duties faithfully. But at length a woman called Zohra, more beautiful than any other woman upon earth, came before their judgment-seat demanding redress against her husband, and the two angels conceived a violent passion for her. On the following day, when she returned with the same petition, they drew her aside and declared their love to her. She replied that she would satisfy their desires if they would do three things : destroy her husband, worship the gods she worshipped, and drink wine. Murderers and idolaters the angels could not agree to become, but they consented to drink wine, " not knowing," says the Persian commentator of the Mesnavi of Jelaleddin Rumi, " that wine was the source of sin and the mother of shame." Then said Zohra : " Every night, by the power of a divine word, ye return to heaven. Teach me also that word." The angels confided to her the secret of God, and as soon as she had heard the word she pronounced it in her turn and rose up into heaven, where God changed her form and turned her into a star. The angels attempted to follow her to heaven, but they were refused admittance. On the intercession of a very pious man, however, they were allowed to choose whether they would be punished in this world or the next ; they chose the former, and now suffer punishment in the land of Babel—whither, if any man have a mind to learn magic, he may go and learn it of them, for they are masters of all magic arts. Tradition says that Mahommad, whenever he looked upon the planet Venus, was wont to exclaim : " God curse Zohra ! for it was she who led the two angels Harut and Marut into sin."

NOTES

The same story, says Rosenzweig, is to be found in the Talmud, where the two angels are called Asa and Asail. The Talmud relates that the angels, after their sin, were carried into a great mountain and suspended by chains over an abyss. It was they who taught Solomon wisdom.

Stanza 4.—For the superstition concerning the origin of precious stones, see Note to Stanza 3 of Poem XXXIII.

XLIII

This ode is inscribed upon the tomb of Hafiz.

THE END

Published by

Facsimile Publisher
Ashok Vihar, Delhi-110052 (India)
Website: www.facsimilepublisher.com

Distributed by

Gyan Books Pvt. Ltd.
5, Ansari Road, Daryaganj, New Delhi-110002 (India)
E-mail: books@gyanbooks.com, Website: www.gyanbooks.com

8 888000 312000